AUNT EDITH

The Jewish Heritage
of a
Catholic Saint

AUNT EDITH

The Jewish Heritage
of a
Catholic Saint

Susanne M. Batzdorff

Templegate Publishers
Springfield, Illinois

Copyright © 1998 Susanne M. Batzdorff

First published in the United States of America by:

Templegate Publishers
302 East Adams Street
Post Office Box 5152
Springfield, Illinois 62705
217-522-3353
www.templegate.com

ISBN: 0-87243-240-8
Library of Congress Catalog Card Number: 98-60893

Manufactured in the United States of America

NOTE OF EXPLANATION AND

ACKNOWLEDGEMENT

You will not find in this book a discussion of Edith Stein's public life nor of her many writings. Edith Stein was a prolific author and translator, and she lectured on a variety of topics to Catholic audiences in various countries. The list of Edith Stein's literary output at the end of this book gives an overview of her published works. The interested reader will find books and articles that address her work in detail. As for me, I have chosen to write about my aunt from a purely personal perspective, to tell the story of her family background and of the relatives who loved her, among whom she lived for a time and whom she loved as well. I have also chosen — and hope not unwisely — to include in the text certain occasional verses which over the years I have composed.

I wish to acknowledge the inspiration of Sr. Josephine Koeppel OCD, who encouraged me to embark on this venture and to carry it through to completion, and the unflagging energy and enthusiasm of my dear husband who was my research assistant, messenger, coordinator of tasks and severest critic. I should also like to thank the Institute of Carmelite Studies who generously allowed extensive quotation from Edith Stein's *Life in a Jewish Family*.

Thanks also go to Hugh Garvey of Templegate Publishers who fielded my questions and concerns by phone, mail and e-mail with kindliness and patience and to Ernst Ludwig and Hannah Biberstein, Rose Garam Batzdorff, and Sylvia Sucher, who read portions of the manuscript and offered helpful suggestions.

TABLE OF CONTENTS

INTRODUCTION

The author of this splendid volume is the niece of a Jewish woman who is considered by the Catholic Church to be a saint. Saints are for Catholics mortal human beings whose lives or, in the case of martyrs, manner of death, the Church considers to be spiritually emulatory. In the case of Edith Stein, a victim of Auschwitz, it was both. Much of this book is a biography, a uniquely precious look at the life and death of a Catholic saint by a close member of her extended and tightly knit family. Beautifully written, it will engross and edify Catholic readers who seek to understand the meaning of sanctity within the context of a very human life, well lived yet tragically ended.

This book is also the biography of Edith's family, most of whom did not convert to Christianity but, like the author, remained believing and practicing Jews, many of whom were caught in the vortex of the Nazi machinery of death. The book is from this perspective not a Catholic book but a profoundly Jewish one. It is the story of a Jewish family, to whom we are introduced living in the main peacefully in the way of the generations of their ancestors that went before them. Their lives were limited and occasionally challenged, to be sure, by the traditional anti-Semitism that would from time to time intrude upon them. But the family was not ground down into desperation. To the contrary, it was a thriving, vibrant human community full of hope, laughter and confidence for the future.

All this was stripped from them by the political and then military success of Nazi racial anti-Semitism which surged through Europe like a flood bursting through the dams of moral and social understandings which had given earlier generations of Jewish families at least some protection when times went bad. This resilient Jewish family, which had overcome so many challenges in the past, could only be swept away like so many other Jewish families. Their story, Edith Stein's story, is a profoundly moving one of pain, struggle, death and survival. Well before the catastrophe, Edith Stein chose, to the consternation of her family and after years of atheism, to become first a Catholic and then a nun, only to be ostracized and finally murdered by the Nazis because to them, she was all and only a Jew. As readers, we have come to know Edith Stein and her family before the catastrophe, and are therefore deeply involved in what happens to them.

This, then, is the context in which those who read this book must encounter the greatness and humanity of Susanne Batzdorff's Aunt Edith. It is an historical and social context fraught with ambiguities piled upon ambiguities, of evils so terrifying that new words which never before existed in human language ("genocide") had to be invented and old words ("Holocaust") redefined even to speak of it, however haltingly and inadequately. When it was over, those who survived would never be the same. Somehow, they found each other, though, and a sense of family returned, defying Hitler's dying hope.

Years passed. A new generation came on the scene. Then a new challenge came, one that would bring the family even closer together. "Aunt Edith" was to be beatified, declared a "Blessed" by the Church. The convert whose defection from the faith of her ancestors had caused her family such pain at the time, was on the path to being declared a Catholic Saint!

10

Sainthood is indisputably the highest "honor" the Catholic Church can bestow upon one of its members. Catholics might think, therefore, that the Jewish community would be pleased by the posthumous elevation of Edith Stein to the ranks of sanctity. But such a presumption, natural as it might be for Catholics, for Jews fails to take into account the complex ambiguities of the Holocaust and the equally complex and ambiguous history of relations between Christians and Jews that went before it.

For Jews, the recognition of the sainthood of Edith Stein by the Church is a challenging and disturbing matter. (Jews and many Catholics reading this use of the term, "recognition," might come to understand that the Church does not "make" saints as one might "make," for example, a papal knight or a cardinal, but simply and with greater difficulty seeks to discern that the deceased is indeed "with God"). St. Edith's niece in this volume eloquently sets forth the Jewish concerns, shared by her family, along with her own reflections. What, Jews ask, are the implications for Christian thought and behavior that might lie beneath the surface of this recognition?

Does acknowledgment by the Church that Edith Stein is a saint mean that only Jewish converts to Catholicism who were victims of the Holocaust were, in the eyes of the Church, true martyrs? Does it portend, therefore, an attempt by the Church to claim the Holocaust, by making Catholics its primary victims? From a Jewish point of view, the six million are all equally victims. One cannot lift one up above the others. All were killed by the Nazis for the same awesomely simple reason: they were Jews. Jewishness alone sufficed to merit capital punishment from the Nazis. What one did, said, had done or might do was essentially irrelevant. Once Edith Stein was put on the train to Auschwitz, she was, whether she wore her religious habit or not, a Jew — slated for that reason to death. So what, Jews quite legitimately ask, is all this about Catholic martyrdom? Convert or not, she did not die as a

Catholic. She died as a Jew, one infinitely precious life among six million infinitely precious Jewish lives. No more, no less.

Secondly, Jews quite legitimately ask, does the Church's recognition of Edith Stein as a saint portend a return to the bad old days? Does it mean that the only good Jew is a Jew converted to Christianity? Will her image as a saint be used to motivate Catholics to seek by fair means or foul (in the past, it is sad to say, the means we Christians used were all too often foul) more and more Jewish converts? Is it her conversion itself that the Church is setting up in the hope that other Jews will emulate it and Catholics organize to bring more about?

In 1987, on the occasion of Edith Stein's beatification, the Bishops Committee for Ecumenical and Interreligious Affairs (BCEIA) of the National Conference of Catholic Bishops issued a statement that was sent to all the dioceses of the United States. The same statement, modestly updated, was sent to all the bishops of the United States in 1997, when it was announced that Blessed Edith Stein was to be proclaimed a saint. The statement reflected and distilled a number of statements issued by the Church hierarchy, especially Pope John Paul II, since the Second Vatican Council. The beatification of Edith Stein, the American bishops said, must not be understood by Catholics as in any sense a triumph of Christianity over Judaism. To the contrary, reflection on Blessed Edith's death can only lead Christians to a profound self-examination of conscience (in Hebrew, *heshbon ha-nefesh,* a reconsideration of the soul) and a profound sense of repentance. Six million Jews, Edith Stein among them, were murdered in countries which had for centuries been predominantly "Christian." Millions of Jews like Blessed Edith were rounded up, crammed into cattle cars, and sent to their deaths by people the vast majority of whom were baptized (though it can hardly be said that they were acting as Christians in those dark days when evil overshadowed the ancient lands of Christendom).

12

Blessed Edith, once she was captured and placed on the train, was treated and killed in Auschwitz as a Jew. Her killers did not consider her Catholicism, only her Jewishness. It is true, ironically, that she might have survived had not the bishops of Holland defied the Nazis and publicly condemned the deportations of Jews. The Nazis retaliated by swiftly rounding up and deporting all of the Jews they could identify who had converted to Catholicism (leaving alone, for the time, Jews who had converted to Protestantism since the Protestant leadership had heeded the Nazi warning to them not to go public with their equally deeply felt concerns for the Jews of Holland). Ambiguity upon ambiguity. Whose decision, to speak out or not to speak out, was the right one for the time? We will never know. But the context, however ambiguous, of Edith Stein being killed for the sake of the witness to her adopted faith, is to the Church more than sufficient to consider her an authentic Catholic martyr even while acknowledging the primacy of the utter Jewishness of her death as merely one Jew equally among six million others. Pope John Paul II made this point forcefully in his homily at the beatification ceremony held in Cologne, Germany, on May 1, 1987.

> Edith Stein died at the Auschwitz extermination camp, the daughter of a martyred people. Despite the fact that she moved from Cologne to the Dutch Carmelite community in Echt, her protection against the growing persecution of the Jews was only temporary. The Nazi policy of exterminating the Jews was rapidly implemented in Holland, too, after the country had been occupied. Jews who had converted to Christianity were initially left alone. However, when the Catholic bishops in the Netherlands issued a pastoral letter in which they sharply protested against the deportation of the Jews, the Nazi rulers reacted by ordering the extermination of the Catholic Jews as well. This was the cause of the martyrdom suffered by Sister Teresa Benedicta of the Cross together with her sister, Rosa, who had also sought refuge with the Carmelites in Echt.

Nor can the beatification or sanctification of Edith Stein give rise among Catholics to thoughts of organizing to convert other Jews. Hers was a unique spiritual journey, a turning away from atheism and back to God in her own personal way. We Catholics can honor her for it. But at the same time we recall that God chose the Jewish people and revealed to them a divine Way (which we call, today, Judaism) which they have faithfully observed since biblical times. To think thoughts of conversionism at the same time as we Catholics meditate upon her life would be to dishonor that life and its death. It would be to ignore the "saving warning," in the Pope's words, that Jewish insistence on remembering the *Shoah* gives to us.

In addressing the Jewish leaders of Cologne shortly before the beatification, Pope John Paul II stated the Church's appreciation not only of Edith Stein but of the fact that the Jewish people, through their faithfulness to Judaism continue to give living witness to the divine revelation given to them as the people of God. He attacked directly the ancient "teaching of contempt" which sought to interpret the destruction of the Temple of Jerusalem in 70 C.E. and the dispersal of the Jewish people (the Diaspora) as divine punishment for their alleged collective guilt for the death of Jesus (an allegation strongly condemned by the Second Vatican Council). Rather than seeing the Diaspora as evidence of guilt, the Church is now directed to understand it as "a phenomenon that has allowed Israel to bear what has often been heroic testimony out into the entire world of its faithfulness to the One God (see the Holy See's *Notes on the Correct Presentation of Jews and Judaism in Preaching and Catechesis,* June 24, 1985, no. VI, 25).

> As early as antiquity, the Jews brought this witness of their faithfulness up to the Rhineland...
>
> Your communities are particularly significant in view of the attempt of the National Socialists in this country to exterminate the Jews and their culture. The existence of your communities is evidence of the fact that God, who is the fountain of life (Psalm 36:9), and whom the psalmist praises as "Lord, Father and Master of my life" (Sirach 23:1), does not allow the power of death to speak the last word. May the one benevolent and merciful Father of life watch over your communities and bless them, especially during the times you are assembled together to hear God's holy word.

14

There is a remarkable confluence of theological insights in this papal statement. First, it can be noted that "heroic testimony" or witness is recognized not only of the Jewish people as a whole over the centuries, but particularly, here, of the Jews of the Rhineland. "Heroic witness," of course, is the precise meaning of the term, "martyrdom." In the first part of this statement the pope is alluding, and not subtly, to the attempt at forced conversion and then massacre (when they refused) of the Jews of the Rhineland by marauding stragglers of the First Crusade in 1096, an attack opposed by the pope and the bishops of the time but one which took thousands of lives. The pope here sees the Christians who perpetrated the event as the evildoers they were and acknowledges their Jewish victims as martyrs for the true faith given by God to Israel. Second, the Pope's prayer for the Jewish community, especially when it is assembled for prayer, acknowledges clearly the validity of Judaism and of the prayer of the Jewish people to the one God who chose them for divine election.

This affirmation of the spiritual validity of Judaism and Jewish prayer, evokes for Catholics the one official prayer for the Jewish people in Catholic liturgy. This is the Good Friday prayer. Before the Second World War, this was a prayer understood as being for the conversion of the "perfidious Jews" (in Latin, *perfideles,* "half-believers," in contrast to *fideles,* "believers," and *infideles,* "non-believers". It was Pope Pius XII who directed that *perfideles* be translated as "unfaithful" rather than "perfidious," which had taken on such negative connotations over the centuries. When Pope John XXIII, of blessed memory, suppressed the term, *perfideles,* altogether, it became in our Catholic missals simply a prayer for the conversion of Jews. With the reform of the Liturgy undertaken by Pope Paul VI following the mandate of the Second Vatican Council, however, the ancient prayer was completely re-written and shorn of conversionism altogether. Now, it is a prayer that the Jewish people remain faithful to

15

the covenant given them by God. In our Catholic tradition we have a saying, *lex orandi, lex credendi,* the Law of Prayer is the Law of Belief, or as we pray, so we believe. It is my argument that one finds in this liturgical tradition a foundational statement of Catholic faith with regard to the Church's attitude toward the Jewish people. Nowhere in our official Catholic liturgy do we pray for the conversion of Jews to Christianity. Rather, the Church calls us to pray for continuing Jewish faithfulness to the Judaism given them by divine revelation.

Here, it might be of help to point out that we have now had more than a decade since the beatification to see just how Edith Stein will be integrated into the Church's memory and teaching. In the numerous references to her in Catholic religious education materials in this country which I have seen, I found a tendency toward neither triumphalism nor conversionism. Rather, she is pointed to as a model of a woman of courage and intelligence, often paired with figures such as Dorothy Day as a model of one who had profound influence on the life of both the Church and of society. Surely, I would argue, this positive record since the beatification should be taken into account by those in the Jewish and Catholic communities who raised these quite legitimate concerns.

The Pope, in his address to Jewish leaders in Cologne and again in his homily at St. Edith's beatification, defined the Church's attitude and intent in recognizing this remarkable woman—scholar, philosopher, theologian, spiritual giant, feminist, and finally, martyr—as a saint. Many in the Jewish community, I well understand, may not agree with the Pope's understanding of Edith Stein as at once fully a Jew and fully a Catholic, but his very sensitive attempt to ensure that her memory will not be abused by Catholics to promote either Christian triumphalism or organized proselytism aimed at the Jews, I believe, should be respected for its integrity within the context of Catholic belief.

16

Pope John Paul II to the Jewish Leaders:

Today the Church is honoring a daughter of Israel who
remained faithful, as a Jew, to the Jewish people, and, as a
Catholic, to our crucified Lord Jesus Christ. Together with
millions of fellow believers she endured humiliation and
suffering culminating in the final brutal drama of
extermination, the Shoah. In an act of heroic faith Edith
Stein placed her life in the hands of a holy and just God,
whose mysteries she had sought to understand better and to
love throughout her entire life. May the day of her
beatification be a day for all of us to join together in praising
God, who has done marvelous works through his saints and
exalted himself through the people of Israel.

Pope John Paul II Homily at the Beatification:

Today we greet in profound honor and holy joy a daughter
of the Jewish people, rich in wisdom and courage. Today
[I] present sister Benedicta of the Cross to the faithful on
behalf of the Church as a martyr and ask for her intercession
at the throne of God...
The fact that Jewish brothers and sisters, relatives of Edith
Stein's in particular, are present at this liturgical ceremony
today fills us with great joy and gratitude...
For Edith Stein, her baptism as a Christian was by no means
a break with her Jewish heritage. Quite to the contrary, she
said: 'I had given up my practice of the Jewish religion as
a girl of fourteen. My return to God made me feel Jewish
again.' She was always mindful of the fact that she was
related to Christ, 'not only in a spiritual sense, but also in
blood terms.' She suffered profoundly from the pain she
caused her mother through her conversion to Catholicism.
She continued to accompany her to services in the synagogue
and to pray the psalms with her...
With her people and 'for' her people, Sister Benedicta of
the Cross traveled the road to death with her sister Rosa.
The Church now presents Sister Benedicta of the Cross to
us as a blessed martyr, as an example of a heroic follower
of Christ, for us to honor and to emulate. Let us open
ourselves up for her message to us as a woman of the spirit
and of the mind, who saw in the science of the cross the
acme of all wisdom, as a great daughter of the Jewish people,
and as a believing Christian in the midst of millions of
innocent people made martyrs...
We bow in profound respect before the testimony of the life
and death of Edith Stein, an outstanding daughter of Israel
and, at the same time, a daughter of Carmel, Sister Benedicta
of the Cross...
When we pay a spiritual visit to the place where this great
Jewish woman and Christian experienced martyrdom, the
place of horrible events today referred to as Shoah, we hear
the voice of Christ. As the bearer of the message of God's

unfathomable mystery of salvation, he said to the woman from Samaria at Jacob's well: "After all, salvation is from the Jews." (John 4:22)

Dr. Eugene J. Fisher, Associate Director,
Secretariat for Ecumenical and Interreligious Affairs,
National Conference of Catholic Bishops

MAJOR EVENTS IN THE LIFE OF EDITH STEIN

1891 Oct. 12	born in Breslau
1897 Oct. 12	entered Viktoria School in Breslau
1908-1911	attended the Oberlyceum of Viktoria School
1911	*Abitur* (Comprehensive final exam) in Breslau, with distinction
1911-1913	Studies at University in Breslau: German Studies, History, Psychology, Philosophy
1913-1915	Studies at University in Göttingen: Philosophy, German Studies, History
1915 Jan.	State Examination in Göttingen, with distinction
1915	Volunteer nursing service with German Red Cross at a Military Hospital in Mährisch-Weisskirchen
1916	Substitute teaching in Breslau
1916	PH D examination in Freiburg, *summa cum laude*
1916-1918	Assistant to Prof. Edmund Husserl in Freiburg
1917	*On the Problem of Empathy*, Doctoral Dissertation, Halle, 1917; various

	scholarly writings, unsuccessful attempts to get a university appointment
1921	Chance reading of the Life of St. Teresa of Avila at the home of her friend, Hedwig Conrad-Martius in Bergzabern; Decision to become a Roman Catholic
1922 Jan.1	Baptism and first communion in the parish church St. Martin in Bergzabern.
Feb.2	Confirmation in the private chapel of the Bishop of Speyer
1923-1931	Teacher at a girls' high school and teachers' training institute of the Dominican nuns of St. Magdalena, Speyer; translations and other writings
	Lectures at educational workshops and congresses in Prague, Vienna, Salzburg, Basel, Paris, Münster, Bendorf
1932-1933	Lecturer at the German Institute for Scientific Pedagogy, Münster1933 April Dismissal from position as lecturer at the Institute by government decree under Nazi regime
1933 Oct.14	Entry into Carmelite monastery of Cologne
1934 Apr.15	Clothing ceremony as Sr. Teresia Benedicta a Cruce
1935 Apr.21	Temporal vows; profession for three years.
1938 Apr.21	Final vows
May 1	Ceremony of the veil
Dec.31	Transfer to Carmelite monastery in Echt, Netherlands
1934-1942	Work on her most important books, *Finite and Eternal Being,* and *Science of the Cross,* as well as many smaller writing projects

1942 July 26	Pastoral letter condemning deportation of Jews was read from all pulpits in Dutch Catholic churches
Aug. 2	Reprisal: Arrest of all Catholics of Jewish descent, 300 in number, including Edith and Rosa Stein. Transfer to transit camp Amersfoort, then camp Westerbork
Aug. 7	Deportation from Westerbork toward the East
Aug. 8	Arrival in Auschwitz; gassing in Birkenau
1962 Apr. 1	Opening of the process for the beatification of Edith Stein by Josef Cardinal Frings, Archbishop of Cologne
1972 Aug.9	Conclusion of the complete diocesan process by Cardinal Höffner at a commemoration of the 30th anniversary of Edith Stein's death in the Cologne Carmel; subsequent transmittal of all documents to Rome
1987 May 1	Beatification of Edith Stein by His Holiness Pope John Paul II in Cologne, Germany
1997 Apr. 8	Vatican announced that the pope had officially recognized the miraculous cure of Teresia Benedicta McCarthy, the final step required for canonization of Edith Stein
1998 Oct.11	Announced date for the canonization of Edith Stein by Pope John Paul II in Rome

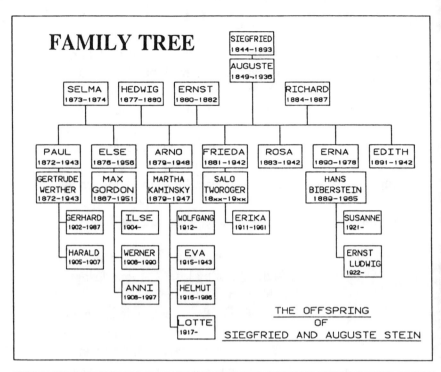

FAMILY TREE

SIEGFRIED 1844-1893
AUGUSTE 1849-1936

SELMA 1873-1874 | HEDWIG 1877-1880 | ERNST 1880-1882 | RICHARD 1884-1887

PAUL 1872-1943 | ELSE 1876-1956 | ARNO 1879-1948 | FRIEDA 1881-1942 | ROSA 1883-1942 | ERNA 1890-1978 | EDITH 1891-1942

GERTRUDE WERTHER 1872-1943 | MAX GORDON 1867-1951 | MARTHA KAMINSKY 1879-1947 | SALO TWOROGER 18xx-19xx | HANS BIBERSTEIN 1889-1965

GERHARD 1902-1987 | ILSE 1904- | WOLFGANG 1912- | ERIKA 1911-1961 | SUSANNE 1921-

HARALD 1905-1907 | WERNER 1908-1990 | EVA 1915-1943 | ERNST LUDWIG 1922-

ANNI 1908-1997 | HELMUT 1916-1986

LOTTE 1917-

THE OFFSPRING
OF
SIEGFRIED AND AUGUSTE STEIN

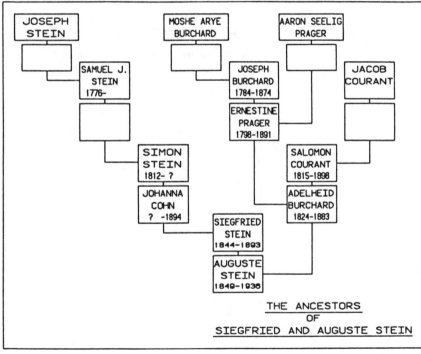

JOSEPH STEIN

MOSHE ARYE BURCHARD

AARON SEELIG PRAGER

SAMUEL J. STEIN 1776-

JOSEPH BURCHARD 1784-1874

JACOB COURANT

ERNESTINE PRAGER 1798-1891

SIMON STEIN 1812- ?

SALOMON COURANT 1815-1898

JOHANNA COHN ? -1894

ADELHEID BURCHARD 1824-1883

SIEGFRIED STEIN 1844-1893

AUGUSTE STEIN 1849-1936

THE ANCESTORS
OF
SIEGFRIED AND AUGUSTE STEIN

PROLOGUE

On a September afternoon in 1933, in Breslau, Germany, I chanced to keep an appointment with Frau Dr. Pietsch-Pietrulla, my dentist, where I was wont to spend far too long a time in the waiting room and pass the long wait perusing the humor column of her sedate Catholic magazine.

Going to the dentist was not my favorite pastime, despite the jokes. But today was different; in the waiting room I found Tante Edith, who was also having a dental appointment. I was delighted to see her there, for I expected that I would have the rare privilege of walking home with her and having her all to myself for a little while. This being her last vacation in Breslau before leaving forever, she had many visitors and was seldom available to us kids.

I had just turned twelve, and we were about to move into a new house. It was a sad time for Grandmother and for us, because we would no longer be living under the same roof, in her big house on *Michaelisstrasse,* where both I and my brother had been born; we would no longer see our grandmother daily, but in addition, she was suffering from a deeper sorrow. Tante Edith, my beloved aunt, my mother's younger sister, and Grandmother's youngest daughter, had just informed her that she would enter a religious order, the Carmelites

23

Eleven years earlier, Aunt Edith had distressed her Jewish family by deciding to become a Roman Catholic, and now this! It couldn't have come at a worse time in history. Hitler had become Chancellor of Germany and immediately begun to implement his fiercely anti-Semitic program. A boycott of Jewish businesses, legislation depriving Jews of various rights previously taken for granted, legitimization of acts of violence against individual Jews, and a constant propaganda barrage in the press and on the radio were making our lives hell on earth. Even those Jews who had barely acknowledged their Jewishness now found themselves clinging fiercely to one another, to seek strength and consolation in the company of their fellows, and that was the moment my dear, sweet Aunt Edith had chosen to sever her ties to her Jewish family. She would become a Carmelite nun, member of a strictly contemplative order, which prevented her from ever leaving, even from visiting her mother, would limit her correspondence and subject it to surveillance by her superiors, would erect a barrier between herself and her sorely threatened and besieged family.

And so we soon found ourselves walking homeward side by side. My aunt's future was on my mind. At home I had been overhearing my parents talking about it, worrying about how it would affect Grandmother, what it meant for the family, whether Edith's decision was indeed irrevocable or whether she might be dissuaded from her plan. I sensed the gravity of her step, but I understood only how deeply hurt everyone was by it and how we all wished she could be made to change her mind. And now, here we were, aunt and niece, walking together so quietly in the still afternoon air. Finally I gathered up all my courage to ask my burning question, "Tante Edith, why are you doing this? Why are you doing this — now?" My aunt with her quiet smile, her severe hairstyle, her dimpled chin, bowed slightly to come closer to her little niece, to try to answer a difficult question. Why? And why now? She must have grasped instantly what lay hidden behind my brief, anguished outburst: Parental conversations overheard, grandmother's silent tears, the whisperings of my relatives, my own terrified experiences of the new wind of anti-Semitism blowing around us in fierce gusts.

It all happened so long ago. I cannot recall the exact words of Aunt Edith's reply, neither did she quote them verbatim in her own account of our talk. It must have gone something like this:

'Susel[1], listen to me. I am becoming a Carmelite, because I must follow my conscience. But that does not mean that I am abandoning you. I will always be part of this family, I will always love you and take an interest in you. I'll write to you and I'll want to hear from you.' I heard her words, but I felt that our relationship could not be as before. I had no words to express my sadness, my doubts, my lack of hope. And what about Grandma? Aunt Edith's thoughts must have traveled along the same path, for at that moment she grasped my hand and held it firm.

"Don't forget to visit Grandma often. She will be lonely when you move away."

'And when *you* move away, too!' I thought, but did not say.

"Promise me," said my aunt.

"I promise."

In recalling this incident, my aunt wrote, "She listened thoughtfully and understood."[2]

But now, sixty-five years later, I am still trying to understand.

TANTE EDITH

A firm handshake,
A cloud-soft voice,
A gentle smile,
But cool, aloof.

Your nephews bow,
The nieces curtsy,
A bit in awe
Minding their manners.

This special aunt
Makes appearances
Only rarely, no more
Than twice a year.

Tante Edith has dimples
In her chin.
Her soft brown hair
Is combed straight back,
A bit too severely.
Are you afraid
To let any wisps
Or curls escape
From the straight and narrow?

In that long-ago time
You kept us at arm's length.
Your time was precious.
You were always writing
Or seeing visitors.
We remained outside
The heavy doors, which
Kept your voices muffled,
Strictly confidential.

Oh, Tante Edith,
We hardly knew you.
Who are you, really?
A mix of theology
And phenomenology?
Of Jewish ancestors
And priestly mentors?

A follower after
Strange gods?
That led you to worship
The Jew on the cross?

Grandmother's favorite,
My mother's playmate.
How do you fit
Into my family?
Where do you belong?

You puzzled your brothers
And sisters,
When you took the veil
Of Carmel.

Grandmother shook her head
And shed silent tears.
Her whole body shook
With soundless weeping
The day you left
To become a nun.

Four decades ago
They killed you in Auschwitz.
You left behind
Books about saints
About philosophers,
Lecture notes, letters.
But no explanations
Of the why and how
Of your life.

The Church is about
To beatify you.
What does that mean
To your Jewish family?

Grandmother could never
Have fathomed such things.
Perhaps she would flee
To the worn, yellowed pages
Of her prayerbook,
To find a psalm
For balance, for comfort.
But now she won't need to.
She's gone, you're gone.
No one is left
To help us, the living
Puzzle it out.

CHAPTER 1

Breslau's History

A Personal Perspective.

Today Breslau, the fourth largest city in Poland, is known by its Polish name, Wroclaw, possibly derived from its Bohemian founder Vratislav I, who died in 921, and officially adopted once again, when it became Polish after the end of the Second World War. It had its beginnings as a Slav market town in the ninth century and was known by its Latin name Wratislavia. The struggle over this town was waged by Polish and German forces over the centuries, but after 1259 it became known as Breslau; it was incorporated into the Holy Roman Empire of Germany[1] and its official language was now German. Its mixed population of Germans, Poles and Bohemians coexisted fairly harmoniously. Under the rule of the Austrian Habsburgs, Breslau took on an increasingly German character. Finally in 1740, Prussia, under Frederic the Great, conquered the province of Silesia from Austria, with Breslau as its capital, and from then on until the end of the Second World War, Breslau was a German city.

Toward the end of World War II, when the battle raged in Silesia, the German government declared Breslau a "fortress" and defended it against the Russian forces to the bitter end. In the final battle, the city was devastated. The surrender of German troops to the Russians took place about a block from the house where we used to live before we emigrated from Germany, on what was then called Strasse der SA, and before that Kaiser-Wilhelmstrasse, (now ul. Powstancow Slaskich), near Victoria St, (now ul. Lwowska). The house in which we lived and the entire neighborhood are gone, destroyed in the fighting. Gone also are the two stately rows of chestnut trees which lined the large garden extending in back of our house, scene of our childhood ball games and other play. Two years ago, tall construction fences barred our view, and when we were there again in June 1997, high-rise apartment buildings loomed in place of our old playground.

When, according to the terms of the armistice agreement of 1945, Silesia became Polish, its capital, Breslau, was given the name Wroclaw. The transformation of the German city of Breslau into the Polish city of Wroclaw was hastened by an almost total population exchange. Most German residents left for various locations in Germany, while Poles, mostly from the city of Lwow, were transplanted to Wroclaw. The change from German to Polish language and culture has had an astonishing impact on this once familiar scene. Returning after an absence of decades and finding these startling changes, one feels a total stranger, and it is only the surviving bridges and churches, the old historic landmarks, that make the strange once more familiar. One finds oneself bewildered in a quasi-dreamlike state.

After wartime devastation and postwar upheavals and transformation, the city has resumed its importance as a center of trade and manufacturing. Its population now exceeds the pre-World War II figure of 600,000. Most of what war had destroyed has been or is being rebuilt. At our most recent visit

30

to the city of our birth we were shown the beginnings of the reconstruction of the "Storch" synagogue, as well as the renovation of my grandmother's home on Michaelisstrasse, now ul. Nowowiejska, both partially supported with funds from the Foundation for German-Polish Cooperation.

What was this city like when Edith Stein grew up, at the end of the nineteenth and in the early twentieth century? Edith was the only child in her family to be born in Breslau. Her own descriptions testify to the impressions this city made upon her in her formative years. In 1900, Breslau had nearly 400,000 inhabitants, of whom 57% were Protestant, 37.5% Catholic and about 5% Jewish. Breslau, the capital of Silesia, was an important economic and cultural center, a railroad junction, banking center, and, with its world-renowned Friedrich-Wilhelm-University, a place of intellectual and scientific progress and prestige. With its sparkling rivers, picturesque islands, verdant parks and attractive suburbs, Breslau was a city where one enjoyed beautiful walks and hikes through the countryside by taking almost any trolley to the end of the line and setting out on foot from there. A level, wooded path alongside the Oder river was a favorite weekend destination. There families walked with small children, enjoyed the peaceful rural environment just a short distance from the noise and traffic of the city and perhaps ended their walk at the *Oderschlösschen*, (little castle by the Oder) and delighted in a light refreshment. We followed that path last summer and reminisced about the days when we went there with our families on Sunday mornings. Edith Stein, too, remembers such outings. She tells of the annual commemoration of Sedan Day , September 2, when "the entire school...would go up the Oder River on a large steamer to *Schaffgotschgarten*."[2]

Winters are long and can be quite severe in Wroclaw. I recall one winter when our school was closed because of cold weather and insufficient coal for heating. The Oder river was frozen for weeks, and the banks of snow that lined the streets on both sides did not melt until March or April. At first brilliantly white, the snow turned into an unsightly greyish and brownish slushy grime. Spots of ice on the sidewalks served us kids as sliding surfaces along which we gleefully slid en route to school. Winter sports were very popular. We ice-skated on the *Waschteich*, a pond in a nearby park where we met our school chums and our cousins for a few hours of skating fun. The former city moat was a more fashionable venue for skating, but we rarely went there. When we returned home from an afternoon of ice-skating, our toes would be frozen and painful, and I clearly remember Mother rubbing my feet, until they revived and, in excruciating pain, I regained the feeling in my toes. Sledding was also a popular pastime, although we had to go some distance to a park that had slopes high enough for real sledding. Later we took skiing lessons, but for real skiing, our Lower Silesian environment did not offer hills high enough. We had to go elsewhere, to the *Riesengebirge* or *Altvater Mountains* to ski. I don't find any mention of winter sports in Aunt Edith's writings. Perhaps they did not play a large role in her youth.

The city's university was originally founded by the Jesuit order in 1645 as the Academia Leopoldina, and gradually expanded, until this development was dealt a severe setback by the outbreak of the Prussian-Austrian War in 1741. The theological college was turned into a military hospital and later a prison, finally a warehouse for food supplies. The Academy resumed its former identity in 1758 as a Catholic institution of learning, but in 1810 it became the *Schlesische Friedrich-Wilhelm-Universität* (Silesian Friedrich-Wilhelm-University),[3] taking over the faculties of Philosophy and Catholic Theology from the former Academia Leopoldina and adding three faculties of the Viadrina University in Frankfurt on the Oder, which had been dissolved: Protestant Theology, Jurisprudence and Medicine. The university grew in reputation and counted many notable scholars among its faculty, among them philosopher W. Dilthey, economist W. Sombart, historian Theodor Mommsen, chemist R. Bunsen, and surgeons J. Mikulicz-Radecki and Rudolf Foerster. Students flocked there not only from all over Silesia, but also from Poland, Bohemia and Moravia.[4] On January 4, 1881, Johannes Brahms conducted his *Academic Festival Overture* for a celebration in the Aula Leopoldina, the famed baroque auditorium in the University of Breslau.[5] Edith Stein fondly recalls her own love affair with her alma mater:

> The old gray building on the Oder (painted yellow a few years ago "in the style of the times") had quickly become home to me. During my free periods, I liked to study in an empty lecture room; there I would seat myself on one of the wide window sills which filled the deep recesses in the wall. Looking down from such a lofty perch at the river and the busy University Bridge, I could imagine myself to be maiden in her castle...[6]

In June 1995, I gave a lecture on Edith Stein in the "Philosophical Seminar" of the University and was told that this was the very room in which she had studied during the first semesters of her university career.

The city boasts several theaters and an opera as well as a number of museums. Its beautiful churches, restored in recent years after the wartime destruction, are a source of pride to the city. Its Gothic *Rathaus* (Town Hall) is probably the city's best-known emblem, appearing on postcards and attracting tourists from everywhere. The visitor to the Historical Museum of Wroclaw located in the Town Hall can now view a bust of Edith Stein among other famous sons and daughters of the city.

In her autobiographical work, Edith tells us of her love for theatre and opera:

> During those years, every time the presentation of a classical drama was announced, it was as though I had been tendered a personal invitation. An anticipated evening at the theater was like a brilliant star which gradually drew nearer. I

33

counted the intervening days and hours. It was a great delight just to sit in the theater and wait for the heavy iron curtain to be raised slowly; the call bell finally sounded; and the new unknown world was revealed. Then I became totally immersed in the happenings on the stage, and the humdrum of everyday disappeared. I loved the classical operas as much as I did the great tragedies. The first I heard was *The Magic Flute.* We bought the piano score and soon knew it by heart. So, too, with *Fidelio* which always remained my favorite. I also heard Wagner and during a performance found it impossible wholly to evade its magic. Still I repudiated this music, with the sole exception of *Die Meistersinger.* I had a predilection for Bach. This world of purity and strict regularity attracted me most intimately. Later when I came to know Gregorian chant, I felt completely at home for the first time; and then I understood what had moved me so much in Bach.[7]

To me, who spent my teen years during the period, such pleasures were barred. Even though we could have attended plays and operas during our high school years, we boycotted such entertainment after all Jewish performers had been dismissed from the stages and concert halls. We ttended only the performances given by the *jüdischen Kulturbund (Jewish Cultural Alliance).*

Breslau also boasts several beautiful parks, with the *Scheitniger Park* (now Park Szczytnicki) the largest and oldest one, originating in the late eighteenth century.[8] Edith Stein recalls strolling there with fellow-students on summer evenings "to hear the nightingales in Scheitniger Park, a beautiful, old English garden in the Eastern part of the city."[9] Just beyond the park is the zoo. The astounding architecture of the *Jahrhunderthalle,* (now *Hala Ludowa)* was notable for its revolutionary design, one of the world's first reinforced concrete constructions. It boasted the largest organ in the world. The interior can hold 10,000 people. This structure still serves as an exhibit space for trade shows and other events. I can remember when the *Stadion* was built in 1928, with its Olympic-sized pool. When we were teenagers, my brother and I would bicycle the long way out from where we lived and spend an afternoon swimming and sunning ourselves. I remember clearly, and with a bitterness that won't fade, the last time we pedaled there and found a sign at the entrance gate that told us: "Juden unerwünscht," ("Jews not wanted here"). We turned right around and pedaled back home, never to return.

After Breslau became Polish in 1945, many beautiful illustrated volumes showing Breslau's picturesque views were published, with captions and text in German; they were eagerly snapped up by nostalgic readers who were now exiled from their home town.

CHAPTER 2

Jewish Life in Breslau

The Jewish history of Breslau stretches back many centuries. The oldest Jewish gravestone in all of Poland, dated 1203 was found in Breslau in 1917.[1] This is the earliest evidence of Jews in Breslau. The medieval Jewish community in Breslau owned synagogues, a ritual bathhouse, and cemeteries. During the fourteenth century, Jews were repeatedly expelled from Breslau. In 1453, forty-one Jews were burned at the stake after having been accused by the Franciscan friar John of Capistrano of desecrating the Host, and the rest of the Jews were driven out of the city. My father would remark that, whenever he crossed the Blücherplatz, (now Solny pl.) he could smell the stench of acrid smoke from the burning flesh of his fellow-Jews centuries before. In fact, in his last long talk with his sister-in-law Edith Stein, Father used his most persuasive arguments to try to turn her away from her plan to become a Carmelite, and this was one of the arguments he brought to bear in his efforts.

In 1455, an imperial decree banished all Jews from Breslau, except those visiting the fair. Even though this prohibition remained in force until 1744, gradually, beginning with the early 16th century, Jews who visited the city to trade at the fairs, sometimes extended their stay for longer periods.[2] As Jews gradually drifted back and proved themselves indispensable to the economy of the region, the municipal council began extending visiting permits to Jews at other times as well. By the late seventeenth century, individual Jews obtained limited rights of settlement in Breslau. The Jews started to organize into a community. One of the oldest Jewish institutions in Breslau was the burial society founded in 1726.

Jews were alternately tolerated or expelled, and their acceptance as residents in a city depended on the whim of the reigning authority. If they were lucky and deemed essential to the economy of the community, they might receive a *Schutzbrief*, a letter of protection. Such a letter might be limited to one person alone, or it might be extended to include his family. It is easy to see that life was precarious for Jews, even with such documents. After Breslau was captured by Prussia in 1741, permission was granted to establish a Jewish community of twelve families. The community acquired a rabbi and in 1761 established a cemetery. As the authorities recognized the importance of the Jews for trade with Poland, they admitted Jewish residents to the city in larger numbers, and by 1776, there were nearly 2,000 Jews living in Breslau.[3]

While in France Jewish emancipation had arrived in 1791, when the National Assembly declared the Jews to be free and equal citizens of the new republic, the Jews of Prussia had to wait until Napoleon's forces conquered Prussia in 1806. One provision in the legal code Napoleon imposed on the vanquished states of Germany provided full equality for the Jews. Napoleon thus became the hero of the German Jews.[4] Yet in the wake of Prussia's humiliating defeat there arose a strident nationalism which found widespread popular acceptance. It led, among other things, to a movement toward improving the physical prowess of Prussian men. Sports and physical exercise were advocated by Friedrich Ludwig Jahn, nicknamed "Turnvater Jahn," (Father of Physical Education).

37

Unfortunately he also preached a fervent nationalistic and xenophobic cult, attacked "mongrelization" of the German race, and these themes of racial bigotry resonated with a demoralized and disenchanted people.[5] The laws imposed by the French victors were revoked soon after the French occupation ended.

At the same time, however, other forces under the leadership of chancellor Karl von Hardenberg strove to modernize the state and introduce measures to break the domination of the feudal landowners and open up the society. Part of this effort was to be the Edict of Emancipation of March 11, 1812 which conferred citizenship on the Jews. It also gave them the right to settle where they chose, the right to buy land, to serve in the army and to marry freely, and it abolished all discriminatory taxes.[6]

This was part of the Prussian reform legislation as a reaction to the devastating defeat it had suffered at the hands of Napoleon.[7] Among the ancestors of Edith Stein's parents, Siegfried and Auguste Stein née Courant (my maternal grandparents) it is recorded that Samuel Joseph Stein, Siegfried Stein's grandfather, received his Prussian naturalization March 24, 1812, while Jakob Courant, Auguste's grandfather, also became a Prussian citizen that year. Joseph Jehuda Burchard, Auguste's maternal grandfather, did not acquire naturalization until March 9, 1837. My father's grandfather Hirsch Biberstein was naturalized on September 22, 1834. No longer were Jews barred from practicing a trade. They could live in any rural or urban location and take employment in schools and municipal institutions. They were, however, still excluded from public office and from receiving commissions in the military service.

The Jewish community reacted enthusiastically to their new status. One consequence was that in exchange for their new rights and privileges, the Jews felt the need to make adjustments in their own attitudes as well. They would henceforth see themselves as a religious community but de-emphasize their "peoplehood" and their cultural uniqueness. Some of the more radical proposals were made by David Friedländer, a member of the Board of the Jewish community of Berlin . He suggested that religious services be conducted in German instead of Hebrew and that all references to the longing for the land of Israel be removed from the liturgy. German culture should replace Jewish traditional values in the schools run by the Jewish community. In 1819 the *Verein für Kultur und Wissenschaft der Juden (Society for Culture and Study of Judaism)* was founded with the stated goal of "the complete revision of Jewish education and Jewish way of life[8]."

The founders of this organization saw the justification of Judaism's continued existence in its contributions to European culture. Their slogan was "Aufgehen ist nicht untergehen" ("merging is not tantamount to perishing"). It is understandable that these ideas were not acceptable to many Jews. There was a distinct rift between the Orthodox and the Reform wing of the community. And yet, although the organization was dissolved five years later, many of its ideas were taken over by the *Jewish Theological Seminary* founded in Breslau in 1854 as well as the Berliner *Hochschule für die Wissenschaft des Judentums*[9] in 1872.

Although the edict of 1812 raised the hopes of the Jews for equal rights as citizens of Prussia, it soon became evident that, even though those rights had been legally guaranteed to them, they could not be taken for granted. The reforms had been imposed from above, and the public did not necessarily support them. Public backlash was vehement, and many people agitated for repeal of the Edict. Despite the Edict of Emancipation, Jewish access to government and military careers was still severely restricted. Many converted to Christianity to gain such opportunities. Social anti-Semitism was still the rule rather than the exception. Many more battles would yet have to be fought to ensure that the privileges given in 1812 would not be retracted or ignored.

After issuing the Edict of Emancipation, the government began to pressure the Jewish community of Breslau to build one large synagogue for congregational worship and to close the small houses of prayer which had sprung up over the centuries. Perhaps the government hoped to be able to have better control over a centralized Jewish community. At any rate, the synagogue *Zum weissen Storch* ("Under the Sign of the White Stork") was built between 1827 and 1829, under the direction of the famous architect Karl Ferdinand Langhans. This building on Wallstrasse 7-9 (now ul. Pawla Wlodkowica) was dedicated on April 10, 1829. However, with the creation of the *Storch Synagogue*, the small "shuls" did not disappear; most remained in active use until 1938.

The *Storch Synagogue* was the liberal synagogue until the so-called *Neue Synagoge* (New Synagogue) was built in 1872. This building, designed by architect Edwin Oppler, was considered the most beautiful after the Berlin synagogue on Oranienburger Strasse. In its ostentatious grandeur it seemed to command homage and respect. It certainly was a center of Jewish existence and a rallying point for the community. Its services were conducted according to the so-called "liberal" tradition, which, to an American reader, may look like a weird mixture of Orthodox, Conservative and Reform practices: Men and women sat separately. The service was conducted for the most part in Hebrew, with only a few prayers recited in the vernacular German and the rabbi's sermon given in German. A famous organ was installed some time during the late nineteen twenties, I believe, and the service was embellished by a great deal of organ music and choral singing. Cantor Borin was famous for his splendid voice. Rabbi Vogelstein, scion of a well-known family of rabbis, was well respected not only in the Jewish community but in the general community as well. His sermons were long and, during the Third Reich, forthright and outspoken. The synagogue *Zum weissen Storch,* more commonly referred to as the "Storch" synagogue, which subsequently served the Orthodox community, still exists and is now undergoing extensive renovations. While the *Neue Synagoge* was burned down during *Kristallnacht,* the Night of Broken Glass, Nov. 9, 1938, the "Storch" was merely vandalized internally, because adjacent houses would have been endangered had this building been set afire.[10]The brutal destruction of the *Neue Synagoge* during the infamous pogrom of Nov. 9-10, 1938, was extremely demoralizing to the Jewish community, even to those who never set foot in this building. To see this solid, venerable structure burn to the ground and its remains dynamited, was a portent of the horror to come, which, until then, had hardly been imagined by even the most pessimistic among us.

Contrary to many published statements, my grandmother Auguste Stein, mother of Edith Stein, did not attend the *Storch Synagogue;* she had her seat in the *Neue Synagoge,* very far back in the women's balcony. It is to this synagogue that Edith would accompany her mother when she happened to be on a visit to Breslau on a festival day. As a teenager, I used to sit by Grandmother's side during the High Holy Days and wonder why she had chosen a seat from which she could not even get a glimpse of any part of the service.

The Jewish community of Breslau became a center of culture and learning with the creation of the Fraenckel Foundation through the testamentary bequest of Jonas Fraenckel in 1846. This enormous bequest helped found the Jewish Hospital, a homeless shelter, orphanage, a home for destitute families and other social institutions. Its most prestigious creation, however, was the Jewish Theological Seminary, which made Breslau one of the foremost centers of Jewish learning in Europe and, until 1870, the only rabbinical seminary in Germany.[11]

41

The *Jewish Theological Seminary* existed until 1938, educating 723 students of whom 300 came from abroad. The course of study for rabbis took seven years, the course for teachers three. Its first director was Zacharias Fränkel (1801-1875).[12] Subsequent seminaries adopted the course of study of this institution as a model for their own institutions.Incidentally, it was in the chapel of the Seminary that Edith's mother Auguste Stein sat with Edith on Shemini Atzeret (the holiday following Sukkot), on October 12, 1933, of which Edith writes in her essay "How I Came to the Cologne Carmel."[13]

The revolution of 1848 was yet another milestone on the road to Jewish emancipation. Jews participated in working for the aims of the revolution, convinced that Jewish equality would come as a result of the political unification and democratization of Germany. Jews felt themselves as Germans and saw their fate intertwined with that of the country in which they lived and which had already bestowed citizenship on them in 1812. Despite this legal victory, their actual status had not changed accordingly and their fond dreams had not been fulfilled. The constitution which was proposed after the Revolution of 1848 and designed to form the basis for a new German nation, stated that "the enjoyment of civil and state rights would be neither conditional nor limited because of religious belief." The Prussian king, however, refused to accept the crown as German emperor from the delegation of the people, and the dream of a unified German nation remained unfulfilled.

Thus the fate of the Jews continued to depend on the provisions of each individual state. In Prussia, which had the largest Jewish population of Germany, 200,000 in 1848, "the Jews were given legal equality in the state constitution of 1850, but their status was somewhat reduced by the declaration that Prussia was a Christian state, which effectively barred Jews from serving as government officials, university professors, and officers in the army. It took another two decades of stubborn struggle before that longed-for dream of emancipation materialized."[14]

After the Franco-Prussian war of 1870-71, the German Reich came into being and the Edict of April 16, 1871 ratified Jewish equality before the law and eliminated the last barriers to Jewish admission to government office. And yet, the reality was otherwise. During the fifty years of the German monarchy, Jews could not become officers and were rarely appointed to teaching positions or higher positions of public office. The social segregation of the Jews was still in evidence. At the university, the fraternities excluded Jews from membership. Consequently, on October 23, 1886 "Viadrina", the first Jewish fraternity, was founded in Breslau.[15] Its primary purpose was the defense of Jewish university students against anti-Semitic insults and humiliating attacks. They practiced fencing and challenged their attackers to duels. Several other fraternities followed suit, and in 1896 an umbrella organization for Jewish fraternities was established. Between 1890 and 1910, twenty-four Jewish organizations came into being for social, charitable, political, scientific and literary purposes; youth clubs, women's groups, sports clubs were also organized.

Legal emancipation and wishful thinking on the part of the Jews combined to nourish the hope for acceptance into the economy, civil service and German cultural life. In retrospect, and after the Nazi persecutions, this hope was revealed as an illusion, but from the perspective of that time, Jewish optimism and hope appeared justified and reasonable. Gershom Scholem, professor at Hebrew University, Jerusalem, and eminent authority on Jewish mysticism, comments in his autobiography:

> The large segments of German Jewry under discussion here, and their intellectual and political representatives, wanted to believe in assimilation with, and integration into, an environment that by and large viewed the Jews at best with indifference and at worst with malevolence.[16]

Born in 1897, Scholem was a contemporary of Edith Stein. His description of mainstream German Jewry may shed a light upon the society in which she, too, grew up:

> At this point I should like to say something about the phenomenon of assimilation which loomed so large in the life of German Jewry in my youth. A great variety of factors were involved there. At the beginning of this century any young Jew who was not part of the strictly orthodox minority faced the progressive deterioration of his Jewish identity ... There was a deliberate break with the Jewish tradition, of which the most varied and often peculiar fragments were still present in atomized form; and there was also a drifting (not always conscious) into a world which was to replace that tradition... The hope for social emancipation (which was supposed to follow the political emancipation completed in 1867-70)-a hope that was largely shared and encouraged by the non-Jewish champions of this emancipation-was in conflict with the general experience of rising anti-Semitism.[17]

Gershom Scholem shocked his friends and family when he emigrated to Palestine in 1923. Zionism was not nearly as popular in Germany then as in Eastern Europe, but gradually it began to gain a following in Germany as well, due to the experience of continuing social exclusion in spite of legal equality. We have already mentioned the xenophobia and chauvinism preached by *Turnvater Jahn* and his ilk. By the latter half of the nineteenth century, racial anti-Semitism based on pseudo-scientific treatises, and envy of Jewish success in the world of business, the arts and the professions had replaced the old religiously based anti-Semitism. Some reputable historians, notably Heinrich von Treitschke, fulminated against Jews. It was he who coined his phrase, "The Jews are our misfortune," later adopted and used ad nauseam by the Nazi propagandists.

Impatient with the disappointing lag between the promising legislation and the continuing persecution and exclusions, German Jews began to pay attention to the stirrings of Zionism. Theodor Herzl's dream for a Jewish homeland did not grow out of religious zeal (he was out of touch with traditional

44

Judaism) but out of his outrage at the ferocious anti-Semitism demonstrated in the Dreyfus Affair[18] in France. In Germany, there could be no Dreyfus Affair, because Jews were excluded from the officer corps. However, it was evident to those familiar with the situation in Germany, that the prevailing sentiments were the same as in France.

The first Zionist Congress took place in Basel in 1897. Young intellectuals founded the Zionist Union in Germany (Zionistische Vereinigung für Deutschland) the same year. Thus Zionism in Germany got its start at the universities, especially in Berlin.[19] But most of its adherents were from eastern Europe. This trend marked the dawning of a suspicion: Perhaps the previously held firm belief in the possibility that Jewish integration and acculturation into the German "homeland" could be achieved without surrendering their identity as Jews might be a delusion, an impossible dream. Perhaps the only solution to the "Jewish question" might be a quest for a Jewish homeland. Nationalism was gaining ground among other European peoples, so why should not Jews follow a similar path? And yet, as soon as World War One broke out in 1914, a great patriotism stirred the Jews of Germany. They volunteered with the same enthusiasm as the non-Jewish men and marched off to war. Edith Stein herself volunteered for service in a Red Cross military hospital so that she could participate in the war effort. Most of her male fellow-students eagerly volunteered for active service, and Edith did not want to be left out. In spite of this widespread patriotic spirit, rumors persisted that Jews were war profiteers and draft dodgers. These slanderous allegations culminated in the insulting and humiliating *Judenzählung,* the census of Jews in military service, to determine the level of their participation.

The results of this survey were never published, because they had revealed a high level of participation and would have been an embarrassment to the instigators of this survey. Even so, the very fact that such a census was taken was the first major breakthrough for the anti-Semitic agitators and had a devastating effect on the morale of the Jewish population. The general impression was one of having been targeted and degraded.[20] After the war, several Jewish organizations published proof that German Jews participated in equal if not greater measure as the rest of the population.

As a result of their wartime participation and sacrifices, the Jews had hoped to be granted complete equality at last, but just the opposite occurred. Anti-Semitism grew much worse. Jews were accused of enriching themselves at the expense of the German people and of being part of an international conspiracy to bring about the defeat of the German army. As a result, the *Reichsbund Jüdischer Frontsoldaten* (National Association of Jewish Front Line Soldiers) was created to combat anti-Semitic threats and to counter allegations about Jewish draft dodgers.

The Weimar Republic brought some changes for the better. It offered Jews opportunities in government service.

> The demand from the time of emancipation that in exchange for admission into German society the Jews should give up their Jewish identity had been largely fulfilled by the end of the Weimar period. The majority of Jewish citizens considered their religion a private affair and lived as Germans in Germany which they considered their homeland. The alienation between Jewish and non-Jewish Germans had disappeared. Jews and gentiles had become indistinguishable. Only the National Socialists reestablished the estrangement by special laws for German Jews and their gradual exclusion and marked the Jewish citizens with the yellow star.[21]

It is typical of the prevailing attitude in the twenties and thirties that the Jewish umbrella organization was named *Centralverein deutscher Staatsbürger jüdischen Glaubens* (Central Union of German Citizens of the Jewish Faith). After the Holocaust, when Jews gradually started to build a community in Germany again, their national organization took the name *Zentralrat der Juden in Deutschland* (Central Council of Jews in Germany),

46

a clear signal that their perception of themselves in relation to the state had changed.

Those Jews who live in Germany and Poland today are, for the most part, not returnées who lived there before the Shoah. A large segment come from the former Soviet Union and are not encumbered by the baggage of those who survived the Holocaust, who were driven out or deported, and who must come to terms with the past in order to build a future in the land of their former archenemy. No matter what their origins, Jews in Wroclaw are today a small minority with few resources. They must find their identity and purpose, found new institutions to replace the ones destroyed and bridge the vast differences among their own communities. The older generation is dying out, and the younger generation for the most part is not educated in Judaic matters, although strongly motivated to learn. Strong and knowledgeable leadership is essential to find among their flock the common denominator and build new communities upon this foundation. During our last visit to Wroclaw and in conversations with the members of its Jewish community, we came away with the hope that young American rabbinical students or rabbis may be motivated to give a year or two of their time to assist these fledgling Jewish communities in finding themselves, to teach them the basics and strengthen their confidence in rebuilding a Jewish future upon this blood-soaked soil.

CHAPTER 3

Ancestors

In her autobiography, Edith Stein meticulously recalls the life story of her mother Auguste née Courant and delves into the past, remembering the two preceding generations of the Courant family. However, when it comes to her father Siegfried, she has almost no stories to tell, no memories to recall. This is explained by the fact that Edith was a baby when her father died and therefore has no personal memories of him. My mother, Edith's sister Erna, who was three and a half years old at the time of his sudden death, sixteen months older than Edith, told me that she, too, had no memory of her father. It is therefore up to us to try to fill in as much as we can concerning the paternal side of her family.

In the nineteen thirties, my father Hans Biberstein developed an interest in genealogy and in the course of his research was able to discover the following facts about Siegfried's provenance: Of Siegfried's great grandfather we know only that his name was Joseph Stein. Joseph's son Samuel Joseph was born in Danzig in 1776 and acquired Prussian naturalization on March 24, 1812. Samuel Joseph Stein's son Simon was born in Langendorf [1] in 1812. We know that he married three times and that his third wife Johanna née Cohn, had seven children, of whom my grandfather Siegfried was the eldest. When we were children, we were amazed to learn that Simon, grandfather Siegfried's father, the one with the three wives, had sired twenty-three children. Perhaps in view of this daunting fact my aunt Edith did not even attempt to tell the story of this tremendous array of uncles and aunts on her father's side but was satisfied to be intimately familiar only with her mother's fifteen siblings.

In addition to the few facts above, we have a treasure in the form of a 27-page long typescript which my grandfather's younger sister Julie Buchen wrote in 1920 and distributed to her nephews and nieces. In this narrative, she reminisces about her childhood in Woiska, "located near the old Jewish community of Langendorf..."[2] She tells us that her father had a farm, but, in addition, he owned a lumber business and traveled a great deal to buy lumber and to deliver lumber to coal mines. In the early 1850s, her father acquired a piece of property in Gleiwitz, with a house on it. It was located near the railroad station, and he started a lumber business with a steam-driven sawmill. With nostalgic affection, Julie describes the flower garden that surrounded this home in which she was born and the small gazebo which was an ideal hideout.

By the time Julie was born, her father had lost his eyesight. Although the family left no stone unturned to obtain medical and surgical help for him, it was all in vain. A touching scene occurred every Friday night:

> Before supper, when our father had returned from synagogue, we children passed in review according to age, he put his hand upon our heads and blessed us without seeing us. Papa was very pious, and our household was strictly traditional.[3]

Julie also tells of the manner in which the religious festivals were celebrated in her home. On the first Seder, so she tells us, brother Siegfried, Edith's father and my grandfather, led the prayers and the reading of the Haggadah,[4] when their father could no longer do so.

Even after he lost his sight, Simon was still capable of estimating the value of a stand of trees by touching the tree trunks and counting their number. He died of a stroke at the age of seventy-two. His widow Johanna was the daughter of a country school teacher and an Austrian mother who died young. Julie remembers that her mother Johanna was beautiful and retained her beauty into her old age. About the marriage of her brother Siegfried, she writes:

> Early in 1871[5] brother Siegfried married Gustel, [Edith Stein's mother] whom we had come to love some time earlier, when she, a niece of Uncle Heinrich, and girlfriend of (my sisters) Emma and Tina, visited our home. We welcomed her warmly as our sister-in-law. Again we traveled to the wedding in our carriage, since the train connections to the little town of Lublinitz were not convenient. Since there were many young people in the family of the bride, the wedding was a lively and merry occasion. Alex [a brother] was employed in a bank at the time and very popular with the girls; I also had a great time. Since I never attended a ball - Mama had grown tired of shepherding my older sisters to parties and claimed that they were not as much fun as they used to be - weddings were the only parties I attended.[6]

Siegfried first met his future wife when she was nine years old. At their marriage, he was twenty-eight, and Auguste twenty-one. The first ten years of their life together were spent in Gleiwitz, where Siegfried worked in the lumber business with his mother. Edith Stein in her book devotes a scant few pages to her paternal grandmother. She was "as strict as she was tender. None of her children dared to contradict her even when she was patently in error".[7] "She entrusted her affairs to a manager who cheated her, and she refused to let herself be convinced by anyone that he was not to be trusted. Consequently my parents finally severed the business connection and left Gleiwitz."[8]

In Gleiwitz, their first six children were born, Paul, Else, Arno and three other children who did not survive to adulthood. In

50

1881, the family moved to Lublinitz, the home of Auguste's parents, where, with the help of the Courant family, Siegfried established his own business. He traded in lumber and coal. Frieda, Rosa, Richard and Erna, my mother, were born in Lublinitz, but Richard died shortly after birth. When the family moved to Breslau in Spring 1890, Erna was six weeks old. Edith, the youngest, was the only one born in Breslau.

Their life in Breslau is recalled in detail in Edith Stein's autobiography, *Life in a Jewish Family*[9]. The Steins made this move, because they hoped for better opportunities for economic progress in the big city and were also prompted by the availability of better schools for their children.[10]

In the first chapter of her autobiography, Edith Stein lovingly sketched unforgettable portraits of her maternal grandparents and great-grandparents in Lublinitz, based on conversations she had with her eighty-three year old mother Auguste in 1933 and on her own memories. Great grandmother Ernestine Burchard, née Prager, 1789-1891, emerges as a pious woman who, even in poverty, always managed to spare a bit of food, a few coffee beans, a cast-off piece of clothing, in order to give to those poorer than herself. Great-grandfather Joseph Burchard was a cantor and prayer-leader and later a manufacturer of surgical cotton. He would gather all male members of his large household and hold services in his home, and he taught his grandsons the Jewish prayers. "He scolded much but never struck any of them. Nor did a child ever leave the house without having received a present."[11] Great-grandfather Joseph lived to be eighty-nine years old, but sadly, in his last years developed into a confused, suspicious man, so that his wife of fifty-eight years could no longer remain under the same roof with him and moved into the home of her daughter Adelheid and her husband Salomon Courant. She lived to the age of ninety-three and was remembered by her granddaughter Auguste Stein, Edith's mother, as a truly pious woman, who prayed with the greatest concentration and

51

intensity both in the synagogue and at the cemetery, as well as on Friday nights when she kindled the Sabbath lights while reciting the blessing. She was accustomed to finish her prayers with the words, "Lord, don't send us as much as we can bear."[12]

Though my great-great-grandmother Ernestine Burchard, nee Prager, died thirty years before my birth, I feel a special affinity with her because of a memento of hers which is in my possession today—a Hebrew-German prayer book bound in purple velvet, gilt-edged and despite its age and wear still elegant. According to an inscription, it was given to her on the occasion of her golden wedding anniversary on December 6, 1866 by the Jewish women's club of Lublinitz. I sometimes have the illusion that my ancestress has just laid this precious book aside and may pick it up again when the time for prayer is at hand.

Edith's grandfather Salomon Courant met his future wife Adelheid Burchard when she was twelve and instantly took a liking to her. Five years later, they became engaged, and they married the following year, in 1842. They opened a little grocery store with a small stock of merchandise and a startup capital of 25 pfennigs, but by dint of hard work and close cooperation they built up their business and brought Adelheid's younger brothers and sisters in to work in the store. Sixteen childrenwere born to them, all but one grew to adulthood. Auguste, or "Gustel," as everyone called her, was the fourth. All the girls were put to work in the store at age four, but also received an elementary education. Gustel was taken out of school when she was twelve, but received private lessons in German and French. The boys were sent out of town to high chool (Gymnasium) and two studied at the university, one became a pharmacist, the other a chemist.

Edith remembers her grandfather as a short, vivacious man who used to hand a bar of chocolate to each child. Since Edith was five at the time of his death, this is the sort of memory she would have of him. He liked to tell jokes and entertain the children in the family, but he was also a capable businessman, highly respected for his honesty and integrity.

After the first World War, a plebiscite was held to determine whether that area would remain German or become Polish. All family members felt themselves to be German patriots and voted for the disputed region to remain German, but the plebiscite went the other way. Bitterly disappointed, they left the town of Lublinitz (now Lubliniec) and some settled in those parts of Upper Silesia that remained German; others moved to Breslau.

For many years, the name Courant was not well regarded in Lublinitz, because of the pro-German stand the Courants had taken in the plebiscite. With the ascent of Hitler, Jews who had remained in the town were deported to the East, and later, during the Communist regime, no one was particularly eager to uncover the traces of this family of Jewish super-patriotic Germans. It is only recently that the town recalled that Edith Stein was the scion of one of their former leading businessmen and pillars of society. Their curiosity was aroused and they discovered under several layers of paint a sign that read "S. Courant." Putting two and two together, some enterprising souls made the connection between S. Courant and the Stein family and began the painstaking effort of restoring the premises. In the summer of 1995, my husband and I visited the Lubliniec branch of the Edith Stein Society and were given a guided tour of the restored house in which the Courants lived and had their business. By the time we visited there, an attractive museum to the memory of Edith Stein and her family had been created. On a large table lay scrapbooks and crayon pictures by local school children on the theme of Edith Stein. They focused on an alleged statement by her that Lublinitz was her favorite town. In an adjoining room we were shown a sofa, a wardrobe and a somewhat dilapidated piano which, tradition has it, were once owned by the Courants. We all sat on great-grandma Adelheid's sofa for a picture-taking session, and, despite a load of eight or ten people, all wanting to be photographed with me on my great-grandmother's sofa, the ancient piece of furniture did not cave in.Edith and her sister Erna spent many childhood vacations in this town.

> For us children it was the greatest vacation treat when we were allowed to visit our relatives in Lublinitz... In that small town we had we were supposed to enjoy ourselves and have a good time. The large house gave us much more space to move around in than the cramped apartment in which we spent our childhood in Breslau. Each room and corner of that house was familiar to us, and every occasion on which we renewed our acquaintance with one was cause for celebration. There was the large store with its enticing jars of hard candies, the ample supply of chocolates, and the drawers in which almonds and raisins could be found. Everything was open to us; but because we were so accustomed to being strictly limited at home, it required repeated persuasion before we felt comfortable enough to help ourselves to anything. Next door was the hardware store which was principally the domain of my uncle. Here, too, there were tempting objects, some of which were usually given to us as souvenirs: pocket knives, scissors, and so on. In later years we were allowed to help out on the weekly market day when the farmers poured in and there were not enough hands to take care of the trade...Occasionally we would take a leisurely walk in the forest and stop nearby to visit the beautiful cemetery where our grandparents were buried, as were, in tiny children's graves our brothers and sisters who had died long before we were born. A trip by carriage to relatives in another small town of Upper Silesia climaxed the joy of our vacation. But what drew us most to return to our mother's hometown was our love for her brothers and sisters.[13]

The city of Lubliniec, which is now all-Polish, is proud of Edith Stein, who, if she were alive today, would not be able to communicate with them except through an interpreter. Still, her memory is loved and venerated, and through her, the memory of her ancestors Salomon and Adelheid. Judging by our own experience, any relative of Edith Stein is warmly welcomed there.

The Edith Stein Society of Lubliniec has as one of its goals the research into the history of the family, and a number of documents throwing light on the business activities of Siegfried

Stein, Edith's father, have already been uncovered.[14] We have already mentioned that the family Stein moved from Gleiwitz to Lublinitz in the fall of 1881. A notice by the Royal District Court states that the firm of Siegfried Stein was entered in the register of business firms on March 23, 1882. An advertisement offers lumber and construction materials and coal for sale at the address of "The old Post Office" where the family lived. The merchandise was stored on a rented lot adjacent to this building. Two years later the family moved to "Villa Nova" a small house with garden which belonged to Auguste's parents and which they apparently made available to the young growing family. By 1884, this was the address given for the firm Siegfried Stein. The "Villa Nova" had been a restaurant with banquet rooms, a bowling alley and billiard room. Parties and performances took place there. Later these facilities were turned into apartments and shops and rented out. Despite many attempts to expand the business and find additional markets, prosperity eluded the firm of Siegfried Stein, and in 1890 the business was sold and the family moved to Breslau. Sadly the hopes for better opportunities in the capital of Silesia were not realized within the lifetime of Father Siegfried. That was to take a great deal of hard work and many years. Not until about 1910 was his widow able to buy the large, comfortable house on Michaelisstrasse, which is still standing, and make it into the home of the large clan.[15]

In his will Grandfather Salomon left the Villa Nova to his son Emil, who moved to Berlin and sold it in 1914. After the plebiscite of March 20, 1921, the town of Lublinitz became Polish, and, as previously mentioned, the Courant family moved away.[16]

CHAPTER 4

The Baby in the Family

"I am not a writer," my mother used to reply whenever we, her children, or others, urged her to write about her life. Or else she would say, "Why should I write about the past? Edith has said it all in her book." Those who knew Erna Biberstein would smile and say, "How typical." She always tended to subdue her own self to the needs and views of those close to her, be it her husband, her more assertive siblings, or later, her children. We know, of course, that all memories are personally tailored and that Erna's reminiscences would differ from those of her sister, though both grew up in the same home and were only a few months apart in age. Yet, although my mother's version of "Life in a Jewish Family" was never written, much of it came to us through oral transmission. Both my parents told us family stories, and I must try to preserve in what I write here bits of my mother's perspective on her relationship with her now famous sister and with other members of her family. My mother did not write a book, but until her death at the age of nearly eighty-eight, she maintained a diligent and faithful correspondence with anyone who approached her on the subject of her sister Edith. She also felt that it was her duty to call attention to any misconceptions or errors in reporting events in Edith's life and background. Only two weeks before her death,[1] in an interview she gave to someone who was gathering data for a biography of Edith Stein, she said, "I have written often to correct misstatements of facts made by various biographers, but no one ever corrected them, and they continue to be quoted."

In my story I shall from time to time refer to such instances, because Edith was intent on pursuing the truth, and my respect for her as well as for my mother directs me to report events as truthfully as possible.

Edith Stein was born on October 12, 1891, which in that year coincided with Yom Kippur, the Day of Atonement. Her mother saw in this a special portent, since Yom Kippur is the most solemn day in the Jewish calendar. The family first lived in a small apartment and struggled with debts and the growing pains of a new business enterprise.

The Stein family had moved from Lublinitz to Breslau in order to improve their fortune, but the sudden death of father Siegfried when the youngest child was less than two years old changed their hopes and plans.

> My father died of a heat stroke on one of his business trips. On a hot July day, he went to inspect a forest and had a long way to go on foot. From a distance, a postman…noticed him lying down but assumed he was simply resting and paid no more attention. Only when, several hours later, he returned by the same route and saw him still at the same spot did the man investigate and find him dead.[2]

Suddenly, not yet forty-four years old, the young widow found herself the head of her household and with the responsibility for the lumber business, which she hoped to transform from a loss enterprise to a profitable one.[3] She had to leave the care of her youngest children to their older sisters.

> My sister Else (then age 17 and studying at a teachers' college) would have to concern herself with the housekeeping and with the children until her younger sisters were old enough to take over these duties. Her management

of the house was so rigorous and her thrift so extreme that everyone came to sigh under her yoke. I was the sole exception since I was but a small child and, so, was still being called by pet names and spoiled with affection; proud of being thus singled out, I was very fond of my beautiful sister.[4]

In her own words Edith creates a most vivid and detailed picture of her early life. She recalls incidents from earliest childhood which are surprising in their exactitude and which led her slightly older sister Erna to wonder many years later (in an interview on Dec. 10, 1977) whether some of those memories might not be based on what Edith had been told by the older family members.

The family first lived in a small apartment on Kohlenstrasse 13, now ul. Stanislawa Dubois, and the lumber yard was established on a rented lot nearby. That house no longer exists, and even Edith had just one memory of it: a big white door which separated little Edith from her big sister Else. Enraged because she could not get to her, Edith drummed against the door in a tantrum.[5] The family occupied a succession of rented apartments, only one of which is still extant. This is the one on Jägerstrasse 5, now ul. Mysliwska. The backyard of this house bordered on the lumberyard on Rosenstrasse (ul. J. U. Niemcewicza). Edith recalls how her mother was able to reach her business by means of a small door which the owner of the house allowed her to put in the wall. However, when the landlord and the woman who owned the property on which Grandmother's lumberyard was located had a falling-out, this vindictive woman insisted that the small door be walled in. As a result, Auguste Stein had to walk the long way around an entire block to get from her home on Jägerstrasse to Rosenstrasse. Thereupon, the benevolent landlord put up a small ladder, so Auguste could get from house to lumberyard, and, a bit later, he made a cut in the wall for her convenience.[6]

As the baby in her family, Edith got a lot of attention. In my mother's words,

> Paul, my oldest brother, carried Edith around the room and sang student songs to her, or...he showed her the illustrations in a history of literature and lectured her on Schiller, Goethe, etc. She had an excellent memory and retained everything. [7]

She was bright and precocious, but perhaps not quite advanced enough to comprehend all that her big brother recited for her benefit.

At any rate, Edith reveals herself as a very sensitive child who suffered from nightmares and even inexplicable fevers as a consequence of upsetting experiences. She got used to keeping her worries and fears to herself. Her mother was busy working all day and came home dog-tired at night. Her siblings did not become her confidants either, not even her sister Erna, who was just one year and eight months older. The children were referred to as three pairs, "the boys,[Paul and Arno]" "the girls,[Frieda and Rosa]" "the children, [Erna and Edith]." Only Else, the oldest girl, stood alone. She was in a category all by herself. She probably appeared as a surrogate mother to the little ones as they were growing up in a household where their mother was overburdened with heavy business responsibilities. [8] Edith and Erna were very close, though very different in appearance and temperament.

> The older sisters used to say she was as transparent as clear water, while they called me a book sealed with seven seals. [9]

Big brother Paul, who gave nicknames to all his siblings, called Edith "pussycat""and Erna "crow." Edith was agile and managed to maintain herself in tussles with the older children. Erna's nickname, Edith believes, had to do with her tendency to get angry and flare up, but her outbursts quickly passed and peace was restored. According to Edith, Erna was conscientious but not overly ambitious. Edith describes her as

59

"pretty, open, and communicative, with deep purity and kindness of heart, exceedingly modest and unaware of her superior qualities, very talented, skilled and adaptable."[10] She criticizes her as being too passive. I dwell on these descriptions with some lingering attention because it is my mother whom Edith describes here. We were fortunate to have her until the age of almost eighty-eight, and we came to admire all her strengths and virtues. Edith could not know, even at the time she wrote this characterization, how these qualities were to be tried and tested, especially in the difficult years of emigration, of starting all over again at the age of fifty, of taking difficult medical state boards in a new country, a new language, cooking and cleaning without the household help she had employed in her former life. At the same time she bore the worries over relatives left behind in a country which plotted and, unbeknownst to her, carried out, their demise.

Eager to learn, Edith was offended when, in spring 1896, it was decided that she should enter kindergarten, while her older sister Erna started school. She had been so used to being lumped together with Erna that she could not accept the idea that now, suddenly, she could not share in her sister's school experience. She rebelled, and each morning she was taken to kindergarten kicking and screaming. Edith, whose birthday was in October, would have to wait until the following April to start school; but that did not suit her. The determined little girl asked for just one birthday present: that she be admitted to school when she turned six in October 1897. Even though Edith could recite long ballads by heart, and could play Author's Quartet (a card game) without any trouble, due to an exceptional memory, she was not yet able to read or write and would be six months behind her fellow-students. Only through her big sister Else's intervention was she granted admission by the skeptical principal, and only on probation, but "by the following Easter, I was promoted with the others."[11]

From then on Edith excelled at her studies, and those who read her reminiscences may be struck by her extraordinary ambition to succeed, by unmistakable signs of pride in her accomplishments which, at times, border on conceit. Edith loved to learn but also loved to show off what she knew. She won praise from her teachers, prizes for her achievements and some envy on the part of her classmates, particularly a cousin, Leni, of the same age, to whom she was often compared. The two little girls were very different in nature, but they were good friends. Only, cousin Leni loved to argue and usually found herself in the wrong. Edith tells us, "On one occasion I remember her becoming very upset and demanding, 'Oh, for once, let me be right.'"[12]

Being part of a large family, with many siblings, cousins and fellow-students, Edith never lacked playmates. Not surprisingly, the lumberyard was a favorite playground.

It was a paradise for children, and when we had no school we were all there as were the many playmates from the apartment house, and friends from school, and relatives as well. There was room for everyone. My mother's dictum was: "Obey absolutely and don't disturb anyone! Provided you do that, you can do whatever else you please." Making a see-saw was the simplest pastime; a plank was balanced on a saw-horse; on either end, a child sat astride the board to bound into the air in turn. We would do this for hours without tiring of it. Playing hide-and-seek was also superb. There were many stacks of wood both high and low. Whatever might be damaged by weathering was kept in sheds. Some of these sheds were several stories high and had stairways; as the interior was dimly lit, one could withdraw into some secret corner to dream or to tell stories.[13]

What my aunt tells about play at the lumberyard is echoed in Aunt Julie Buchen's reminiscences about the delight her own generation took in the ambience of the lumberyard:

Amongst all our friends the story went, "Nowhere can you have so much fun playing as at the Steins," and they gathered at our place every free afternoon... We found the environment of the sawmill fascinating. In the middle of the big loft, a device moved the wooden logs through a machine, cutting them lengthwise in various widths. We kids had fun seating ourselves on the ends of the logs and riding along. You could imagine you were travelling somewhere. The sound of the saw still rings in my ears, and the scent of the sawdust remains unforgotten, so that whenever I pass a sawmill, I feel nostalgia for my lost home.[14]

As for me, I can corroborate similar sentiments from my own memories. We, Edith Stein's nieces and nephews, together with *our* school friends, also enjoyed those same games and sports at the paradise that was Grandmother's lumberyard. The rules had not changed, the fragrance of lumber and sawdust is still in my nostrils and the memories of us kids tumbling around among the stacks of wood we climbed are easily evoked. When I think of the lumberyard, I also see before me my grandmother. She kept a sizable vegetable garden in one section of the lumberyard. There one could find her, bent over the vegetable beds, pulling a carrot , rinsing it under the water pump, then handing it to me as a fresh and fragrant treat. At other times, we would be pressed into service by Aunt Frieda, Grandma's bookkeeper, to help harvest strawberries. One early memory is of an afternoon when I was playing at the lumberyard, when a heavy rainstorm burst through the clouds. Uncle Arno, who was the business manager, determined that I could not be sent home in this storm, and Herr Latwin, a hired hand, was delegated to carry me home, a distance of perhaps a mile, under a large umbrella. He wore high boots, so that the deep puddles through which he had to wade did him no harm, and for me, the whole adventure was a lark.

In the summer of 1997, my husband and I searched out the site of the lumberyard, which is now a somewhat run-down lot, with a shed and some heavy equipment signaling the approaching demise of the weeds and wild poppies growing there, faint reminders of Grandma's garden. It appeared likely that this space is being reclaimed for some commercial enterprise in the near future. There was no one around to ask about these plans, and it wouldn't have mattered to us anyway, for the past was gone, the cast of characters had vanished long ago. Not even the scent of sawdust lingers, and the ghosts of yesterday were visible only to me.

CHAPTER 5

Adolescence And High School Years

Some years after I got married, my mother gave me an heirloom of sorts, a hand-embroidered tablecloth. Not just an embroidered tablecloth, but a tablecloth with a history. Mother related how she and her sisters had worked on it together for their eldest sister Else's trousseau. I have since passed this table-cloth on to Aunt Else's great-granddaughters who live in Israel and who never knew her. Our family, like so many Jewish families in the Hitler years was scattered over many parts of the globe. My aunt Else, her husband Max Gordon, and their daughters Ilse and Anni went to Colombia, South America in 1939, where their son Werner had preceded them more than ten years earlier.

The excitement with which the family prepared the trousseau for Else's wedding is described by Edith. Max Gordon announced his engagement to Else, Edith's eldest sister, by special delivery letter in September 1903. Since the engagement lasted only two months, and since Else herself remained in Hamburg where she taught at a private school, the family in Breslau "worked on her trousseau with feverish activity and immense pleasure."

Catalogs were studied, and many things were bought ready-made; but even more were sewn at home. A seamstress came to the house, and in her capable hands, linen, damask, and Swiss-embroidery were transformed into marvelous creations...We were allowed to help, also, when we were not in school. At times, even some of our cousins joined in. When that happened we all sat in a large circle sewing and embroidering while one of us read something humorous aloud.[1]

It pleased me to imagine that scene while looking at the above-mentioned tablecloth. News of their impending marriage was greeted with great joy. Else was an attractive young woman, who had had many admirers, but she was also restless. Max was a cousin of my grandmother, a dermatologist practicing in Hamburg. He was nine years older than Else. had a wonderful sense of humor and got along well with friends and family. Since Max Gordon disliked traveling, the wedding took place in Hamburg, and the family could not attend. Grandmother went to Hamburg by herself, quite reluctantly, because neither bride nor groom could be persuaded to have a religious ceremony. It did not take long, however, until the young wife expressed great homesickness for "the children." Her husband was perplexed, because she was then pregnant with her first child. However, he soon discovered that it was her youngest siblings for whom she longed, and he readily agreed for her to invite them for a visit during the next summer vacation.

This trip to Hamburg was a great event for us. Never before had we gone so far away; besides we had not even met our brother-in-law as yet. We had every reason to be charmed by him. He received us with brotherly affection and plied us with attentions.[2]

Hamburg offered the two girls an adventure in sight-seeing and unaccustomed treats as well as the attentions of their witty, benevolent new relative. It is perhaps this image that Edith recalled when, a few years later, in spring 1906, she wanted a break from her life as a schoolgirl. Having spent nine years as a student, she announced to everyone's surprise that she wanted to quit school. Her mother did not try to dissuade her:

> "I won't coerce you," she said, "I allowed you to start school when you wanted to go. By the same token, you may now leave if that is what you want."[3]

Spending that time with her big sister and her family in Hamburg made sense. Else loved her "baby sister" deeply and at that time could well use a helping hand with her busy household, a toddler and a newborn son. Originally only a six-week stay was contemplated, but it extended to ten months. Edith worked hard but also enjoyed a new camaraderie with her much older sister and the change from the regimented school life to which she had been accustomed. "I almost believe that the days I spent with her were the happiest days of my sister's marriage," says Edith.[4]

Her brother-in-law Max Gordon was something of a maverick in his professional life. Increasingly over the years, his antagonistic stance toward health plans and resistance to new treatments, e.g. Salvarsan for syphilis, isolated him from his professional colleagues and created animosities and confrontations. Gradually his medical practice dwindled.

Away from her mother's home, Edith found herself questioning some of the traditions with which she had been raised until then. Gradually during those months, her adolescent individuality began to unfold:

> My existence in Hamburg, now that I look back on it, seems to me to have been like a cocoon stage. I was restricted to a very tight circle and lived in a world of my own even more exclusively than I had at home. I read as much as the housework would permit me. I heard and also read much that was not good for me. Because of my brother-in-law's specialization, some of the books that found their way into his house were hardly intended for a fifteen- year-old girl. Besides, Max and Else were totally without belief; religion had no place whatsoever in their home.[5]

In a letter to Sr. Waltraud Herbstrith OCD, Ilse Gordon, eldest daughter of Max and Else, comments: "It is true that my parents did not attend synagogue and did not observe the traditional forms of the Jewish religion at home, nor educate their children in accordance with them. Yet I myself have a different concept of religion, which goes far beyond these forms and which, I suppose, I got from my parents."[6]

Edith continues her reflection by saying: "Deliberately and consciously, I gave up praying here."[7]

From this one sentence, several biographers and commentators have deduced that Edith Stein became an atheist at age fifteen. I would submit that this gives too much weight to one brief remark. First of all, Edith only tells us that she stopped praying. We do not know what sort of prayers she had been accustomed to until then. Were they the prayers of childhood, which would suddenly no longer appear meaningful or appropriate to the adolescent away from home for the first time? Besides, a thoughtful young woman, who is searching for the truth, as Edith was fated to do all her life, is bound to struggle with doubts and uncertainties, especially during her teenage years. In the process of growing up, Edith was destined to experience a number of shifts in her thinking. That a fifteen-year-old does not pray is probably much more common than that she should observe this fact in herself and comment upon it.

At any rate, her ability to take a more objective look at the tradition in which she had grown up, enabled her to take a more detached view toward the things of mind and spirit. This tendency would develop ever more strongly until, as a university student of philosophy, she would examine all concepts hitherto taken for granted under the exacting lens of phenomenology, subjecting them to a severe test of observation and critical judgment.

A crisis in the family brought Edith back to Breslau, the critical illness of her brother Paul's two-year-old son Harald. He had come down with scarlet fever, and the whole family hoped that Edith could nurse the little patient back to health. Sadly, he died a few days later.When Edith returned to Breslau after an absence of ten months, she was once more extremely goal-oriented, and with the help of tutors in math and Latin, managed to pass the entrance examination for the upper level of *Gymnasium* (Secondary school). During those months Edith really discovered her passion for learning. With a keen eye and with humor she observes her tutors, acknowledging their strengths and weaknesses and probably taking away some valuable lessons for her own later teaching career. By April Edith was ready for the entrance examination and was admitted to *Obersekunda*, the seventh year of secondary school.

"So I became a student again," she says, and it appears clear that, as a student, she feels in her element.[8] Soon she was once again one of the top students. Her eagerness and ambition and her sometimes very obvious joy at excelling do not seem to have alienated her from her fellow-students, for she made a number of new friends. Years earlier, her aunt Cilla had called her a "Streberin" (go-getter).[9] This was meant as a compliment, but Edith resented it, as she always believed that being good was superior to being clever. The conflict persisted throughout her life, I believe. On the one hand, Edith delighted in intellectual triumphs and achievement, on the other, she bent her efforts toward humility and modesty, from childhood until her life in the Carmelite community. Her oft-quoted statement, "What was not according to my plan, was part of God's plan," might be cited here. A less resigned, less faith-based view might be that Edith Stein's aims for a university career were thwarted because, in her lifetime, the prejudices against women and Jews stood like an immovable wall between her and academic advancement. Her doctorate, passed with highest honors, her early successes in her field, her acclaim as a lecturer, her diligence as a translator and author, were all nipped in the bud, and her future in all these areas cut off. Her hopes for a happy marriage came to naught as well, although her reticence provides little information on this private aspect of her life. Was the road to Carmel then part of "God's plan"? And even more problematic: Was her death in the gas chambers of Auschwitz part of "God's plan"?

Let everyone reflect on these ideas and draw his or her own conclusions.

CHAPTER 6

My Grandmother, The Matriarch

Elsewhere in this book, I have already spoken much of my grandmother, the "great woman," of whom so much is told in the writings of Aunt Edith, who was her youngest daughter. Physically, Auguste Stein was short, a bit on the round side. Like most widows in her time, she always wore black, and, at home, she never appeared without an apron. When I think of her in repose, I see her sitting by the window, where she could watch the world passing by, the trolley, vehicles and people. Her ever-present knitting in her hand, she would converse with us or read. But that was not her typical attitude. Most of the time, even as an octogenarian, Grandmother was busy, walking to and from work, inspecting how matters stood at the lumberyard, bending over her vegetable bed, or negotiating with customers.

Early in the morning, she liked to comb and braid my hair. I would sit and sing all sorts of tunes, while she was busy running the brush and comb through my thick, black hair to tame it and make it shine before winding it into two long braids that hung over my shoulders and down almost to my waist.

When I demonstrated my total lack of dexterity in knitting socks, a school assignment which I detested, she would quickly pull the whole mess out of my hands and, a bit contemptuously, say, "Here, let me finish that!" The full-length stockings she knitted for her grandchildren, usually made from rough greyish wool, were not favored by us, because they scratched and itched; yet for the sake of peace in the home, once grandmother completed them, we had to wear them.

In our younger years, Grandmother often gave a hand with our weekly bath. Here is how my brother Ernie describes these scenes:

> When she bathed us kids, as happened quite frequently when we were very little, she entertained us with songs from operettas by Jacques Offenbach ("There came a rich Brazilian planter"...) and other show tunes from her youth. At the conclusion of the bath, she wrapped us from head to toe into gigantic bath sheets and pretended, while drying us, that we were mountains of dough which she had to knead into bread. That proceeded with lots of tickling and pinching, until we were totally out of breath with laughter, Grandmother no less than we.[1]

Yes, Grandmother had a vibrant joie de vivre, an unflappable sense of humor which must have helped her conquer many hardships in her life. As a child she had taken piano lessons; decades later, she still remembered a few bars of Strauss's waltz, *"Wine, Women and Song."* On her seventieth birthday, she danced the waltz with her oldest grandson Gerhard Stein and on my parents wedding feast she danced with her new son-in-law Hans Biberstein.[2] Though she was not highly educated, she had very good common sense and great business acumen.

She was born in 1849 to Salomon and Adelheid Courant, the fourth child in a family of fifteen. Edith tells us in her autobiography:

> All the daughters were expected to do chores as soon as they were four years old. They helped in the store which expanded with each new year. They were taught the household skills and later took turns managing the house; In addition they also learned to do needlework. The older children received their elementary education in the public

71

schools. (From the age of five my mother attended a Catholic elementary school.) Later my grandfather started a private school for his four eldest and for the children of three other Jewish families. My mother was taken out of school when but twelve years old, to help in the household; however, she was given some private lessons in German and French... Religious instruction was imparted to them by Jewish teachers in school. They were taught a bit of Hebrew, but it was too little to enable them to translate on their own so as to pray with understanding. The commandments were learned, parts of the Holy Scripture were read, some psalms were memorized (in German). My mother says she attended these instructions with liveliest enthusiasm; and, also, that it had been impressed on them to respect every religion, never saying anything against one that was unfamiliar to them. [3]

At the age of eight, Grandmother was capable enough to be sent to out-of-town relatives to help out in an emergency. Her uncle esteemed her highly and liked to take her with him to market to be his cashier when he sold his merchandise. For her efficient help he would reward her with lavish gifts. But one time, when she overheard him speaking ill of her parents, she left the market abruptly and returned home, hitching a ride in someone's carriage.

Even as a little girl, she did not shy away from hard work. On laundry day, she insisted on helping the maids in the house. At age ten, she would rise before dawn with them and rub her hands raw with the strong soap, without complaint.

Grandmother's home was in Lublinitz, a town in Upper Silesia not far from the border. Even though Auguste left the parental home at the time of her marriage, at age twenty-one, that place remained "home" to her for the rest of her life. After the First World War, Lublinitz's future was determined in the hotly contested plebiscite of 1921, in which the Courant family earned the hostility of their Polish neighbors by their staunchly pro-German partisanship.

As I mentioned earlier, my grandmother first met her future husband Siegfried Stein when she was nine. Apparently Grandfather's mother Johanna Stein was a bossy type, and her children were afraid of expressing an opinion that differed from

72

hers. However, she appreciated and liked Gustel and learned to value her sound judgment; she respected her opinions and willingly listened to her point of view.[4] One such time when Gustel dared to interfere in family matters was in behalf of her brother-in-law Leo Stein. His mother felt that he disgraced the family because he was an aspiring actor. In fact, when his mother kicked him out, his sister-in-law took him in. She believed in his talent and therefore championed him and tried to mediate between him and his mother. Subsequently he became famous as a playwright and director of musical comedies. During a recent visit to Berlin, a young relative pointed out to us the elegant villa in which he and his family used to live in a fashionable part of town. His only daughter Hanna died only a few years ago.

The lumber business in Gleiwitz which Johanna Stein owned and where her son Siegfried was employed was not a success. Of necessity, Siegfried and Auguste decided to leave and moved with their already numerous family to Lublinitz, where Auguste's parents lived. With their help, the young people started their own business. This proved to be a difficult undertaking with many setbacks and it repeatedly required substantial help from Auguste's parents, Salomon and Adelheid Courant. Besides the frequent business reverses their life was beclouded by the tragic deaths of four of their children. Grandmother bore eleven children altogether, of whom seven reached adulthood. The house they lived in belonged to the Courants. It was small and attractive and had a large garden. I suppose from that time stems Grandmother's hobby of growing fruits and vegetables. She enjoyed planting and tending her crops and distributing some of her bounty to friends and acquaintances round about. She also planted a row of apple trees, but by the time they bore fruit, the family had moved on. Edith recalls that later, when returning to Lublinitz for vacations, she and her siblings were allowed to play in the orchard and pick as many apples as they wanted. In 1890, the

73

Stein family moved to Breslau. Starting over in a new environment proved difficult.

Feeding the family became a real problem; the new business, burdened with debts, took a long time in getting on its feet. My mother never said a word about the difficulties she had in her marriage. She has always spoken of my father with a warm, loving tone in her voice; even now, after so many decades, when she visits his grave, one can see that she still grieves for him. Since his death, she has always dressed in black.[5]

In reading these lines, I am puzzled. Do they indicate, in a subtle way, that my grandmother had marital difficulties, but did not speak of them? Or do they imply that there were none? I can only say that, like my aunt, I never heard her complain about her husband or mention any faults he might have had. On the other hand, I have wondered at times about how little this grandfather was mentioned altogether. By contrast, my paternal grandfather's name often came up in conversation, and though Father, who was an infant at his father's death, had no memories of him, he had received from his mother a very real image of his father. She talked about him often and affectionately, and a large portrait of him hung in her living room. Of course, this does not prove anything as far as the marriage of my maternal grandparents is concerned. What we may safely assume is that Grandfather's business acumen may not have been equal to his wife Auguste's, and that she may have come to realize in later years, when she took over the lumber business after her husband's sudden demise, how much better she was able to manage it than he could. And with that might have come the realization that the early years of hardship and poverty could have been avoided, if her husband had been a more capable businessman.

I have already spoken of the tragic death of Grandfather Siegfried Stein on July 10, 1893 and the tremendous upheaval this event caused in the large family. At the time of the funeral, all the relatives offered sage advice. They counseled

74

Grandmother to sell the indebted business and rent a larger apartment where she could live with her brood and rent out rooms to gain a little additional income. Her brothers would help out if necessary. Grandmother was not at all thrilled with this plan. She made her own plan, which was to apply her efforts to putting the lumber business back on track and turning it into a profitable enterprise. Despite the severe loss she had just suffered, she was confident that it could be done and that, with the help of her older children she would succeed. Her task was far from easy. She had to feed her family, send the children to school and pay all debts. Her business ethics were those she had learned at her parents' knee, and they demanded that she first pay all obligations. At that time, she could not afford to finance a higher education for her eldest son Paul, who was just 21. He had completed *Gymnasium,* but, although he was a bookish type with a real zest for learning, he would have to earn his keep. The oldest daughter, Else, was in charge of the younger children but also attended a teachers' college.

Next in age was Arno, who, at the time of his father's death, was not quite fourteen years of age and still a schoolboy. His mother decided to let him learn the lumber trade so he could enter the family business. After serving an apprenticeship in a lumber firm and getting some general business training, he entered his mother's firm, learning the trade from the bottom up, advancing step by step until in the nineteen thirties he became head of the firm. Although his tendency to fly into a rage caused conflicts between him and his mother at times, he worked side by side with her for all those years and maintained his love and respect for her.

While exalting the virtues of my grandmother, it is incumbent upon me, for the sake of truthfulness, to mention one less positive trait which all who knew her had to acknowledge: She somehow came into conflict with every one of her children-in-law. Edith Stein tends to put the blame on her

75

brothers, for the unfortunate choices they made when selecting wives for themselves.

> Paul was very young when he secretly became engaged. For years he carried on his courtship with his betrothed against my mother's will; and finally, since he still could not get her consent to the engagement, he furtively left home. My sister Erna and I were still children at the time. We awoke one night and saw Mother weeping. We ran to her, climbed on her lap, and tried to comfort her. Only years later did we learn that that was the very night on which my eldest brother was discovered to be missing; and our other brother and sisters were out looking for him. He had followed his fiancée to Berlin and wrote only after his arrival there. They were married; we celebrated the wedding as a family feast; the young couple was supported in every time of need, as a matter of course; the eldest grandchild was given the most loving attention; but a cordial relationship with her daughter-in-law never developed, even though Trude, my sister-in-law, tried again and again to bring it about.[6]

For another slant on this relationship, here is what Paul and Trude's son Gerhard wrote in October 1984:

> When my father dated my mother, she overcame her shyness by writing to him that she considered herself engaged. Unfortunately, my grandmother Auguste Stein and my mother did not harmonize because of their different abilities and interests. My grandmother was primarily a business woman and very particular about her household. My mother's strength was in the arts and sports, while her household became secondary to this. One of her hobbies was raising canaries in her kitchen.
>
> Grandmother's dislike of my mother went so far that she asked my mother personally not to marry my father.[7]

The reason for Grandmother's violent objections to this match is not clear from the above quotations. Obviously the temperaments and priorities of these two women differed greatly, but could that have been an impediment to allowing this marriage? I recall that my grandmother was critical of Trude's housekeeping; she would not drink her coffee, and when invited to her home for a birthday celebration, Grandmother made sure that her daughter Rosa brought her specialty, *Streuselkuchen,* so that Grandmother would not have to eat the cake which Trude had baked and in which she had little confidence. Grandmother was quite merciless in ridiculing this daughter-in-law. By contrast, I never heard Aunt Trude speak of Grandmother in any manner other than with deep respect and even affection. Altogether I would agree with her son Gerhard, who says, "My mother had a heart of gold."

Next Aunt Edith tells the story of Arno's bride:

> My brother Arno chose his bride with the approval of my mother and all of us. A classmate of my sister Else's at the teachers' college, she had long been a friend of the family. When still very young, she had gone to America with her family, married there, but later had the marriage annulled. She earned her own living and used her savings to travel to Germany to visit my sister in Hamburg and us in Breslau. Very merry, noisy and vivacious, she always brought a good deal of life into our quiet house. Probably she set her sights on marrying my brother long before the thought occurred to him. She was overjoyed when her wish became reality. The family, in turn, happily received her; the young couple even moved into our house which had just been bought. Indeed, for a while, an attempt was made to run a kind of joint household. But here, again, it was impossible to achieve a harmonious co-existence. What irritates my mother most about both of my sisters-in-law is that neither one has learned how to run a well-ordered home. One of them, musically talented, spends a great deal of time taking or giving music lessons. The other one loves to go shopping and visiting and she constantly seeks new stimulation outside the house. Both are thoroughly incompatible with my mother. As kind and ready as my mother is to help anyone at all, there are some character weaknesses for which she had no patience whatever: these are, above all, dishonesty, tardiness, and an exaggerated self-importance.[8]

When her own daughters told her, half in jest and half in earnest, that she made a poor mother-in-law, she was very distressed. Edith, however, observes that her family had such an individual character that it would be hard for them to accept outsiders into the fold. She quotes a favorite expression of her mother and her sisters Frieda and Rosa, "These people are altogether different from us." Such a pronouncement signaled a definite demarcation. The small annoyances stemming from these differences in their temperament and makeup apparently

77

fueled a constant climate of irritability and conflict which were detrimental to domestic tranquility *(Shalom Bayit)*, a very important concept in Judaism.

My cousin Lotte Sachs, the youngest daughter of Uncle Arno and Aunt Martha, wrote to me just recently:

> ...I'm just re-reading *Aus dem Leben einer jüdischen Familie (Life in a Jewish Family)*; my reaction to some of the passages is much stronger now than it was when I read the draft in German years ago...and later the English edition. It seems incredible to me *now* that Aunt Edith wrote about all the "warts" of the family in such a very direct way; even though the book wasn't published till after the siblings' passing, we, the next generation, might still be suffering.[9]

We were particularly close to Uncle Arno, Aunt Martha and our four cousins, their children. Despite our age difference, we played together in the back yard and were invited often to the garden they owned at the edge of town. That garden was a veritable children's paradise. Even though we were always drafted to help with weeding, watering and harvesting of a multitude of vegetables, there was plenty of time for play, and often a trip to the nearby Oder River afforded opportunities for a dip in the muddy and very likely polluted water to cool off on a hot summer day. Housekeeping in the ramshackle cabin was more than casual, which suited us children to a tee. A primitive cookstove, a couple of bunk-beds, some straw mattresses and a battered volume of James Fenimore Cooper's *Leatherstocking Tales* made overnight camping, while not exactly a luxurious experience, at least a possibility. We generally did not spend the night, but went home at the end of a day tired, dirty and laden with asparagus, strawberries and garden flowers, which we proudly carried back to our parents.

Uncle Arno, of course, also presided over the lumber yard, where we would encounter him at work, clad in rough work clothes, his tweed pants stuffed into long heavy socks. As he clambered about among stacks of lumber or shouted instructions to his employees, he looked very impressive to us kids, probably a lot more impressive than Aunt Frieda, who sat behind a desk in the dark *Kontor* [office] or the small woman with the white hair, my grandmother, who was the "boss-lady". I cannot help comparing Uncle Arno's competent self-assurance in the realm where he belonged with his existence in New York after his emigration from Germany in 1938.

Both Arno and Martha continued to maintain close ties to us, and it was a special delight for my uncle to show us New York when we arrived in February 1939. He, having arrived about four months earlier, felt like a native and proudly took us around to see the sights.

Uncle Arno had a difficult time adjusting to life in America. He had been used to hard work and meaningful activity and now he felt lost in the big city and was never quite able to gain a foothold or build a meaningful existence in the New World. He acquired a small concession stand in an office building on Union Square, where he sold newspapers, magazines, candy and cigarettes. His wife Martha had taken a job as a live-in housekeeper and governess to a wealthy businessman's family; thus, the Stein couple could not live together and reestablish a home life. Their children were grown and scattered, and their one daughter Eva had to remain behind in the clutches of the Nazis. Later, the couple moved to San Francisco, where their son Helmut lived with his family and where Arno and Martha could be together once more, living in retirement; but since both were ailing, it was a period of decline for them. They were able to enjoy their grandchildren in San Francisco and occasionally visit in Atlanta, Georgia, where their daughter Lotte, a trained nurse, lived with her husband and two boys. Wolfgang, the oldest son and his wife at first struggled to farm on an unproductive piece of land in North Carolina, but later moved to Utica, New York, where my cousin took a factory job with regular hours and a weekly paycheck.

Wolf and his wife Ilse were among the relatives who witnessed the beatification ceremony of Aunt Edith on May 1, 1987.

Uncle Arno's older sister Else had married Max Gordon, who was actually a distant relative of my grandmother. Since they lived in Hamburg, they were spared the daily irritations that contributed to the in-law problems in Breslau. Aunt Else's husband, a dermatologist, was quite a bit older than she, and they had three children. Edith Stein, in her book *Life in a Jewish Family,* gives a detailed account of Else's marital problems during the early years of her marriage. By the time this book was published, Max and Else had died, and so the airing of their "dirty linen" for all to see was deeply troubling to their offspring. In a letter dated March 5, 1988, my cousin Anni wrote to me:

> It contains too many things which do not concern the public and can be seen onesidedly. In my English translation, *(Life in a Jewish Family)* I have inserted slips with data which I myself remember, and with corrections [for my family].

My brother and I have fond memories of a visit to Uncle Max and Aunt Else in Hamburg. Hamburg was a beautiful, cosmopolitan city, with two scenic rivers, the Elbe and the Alster, and our aunt could not do enough to show us the sights of the city and its environs. My uncle, who had a great sense of humor, treated us to all the parodies, stories and songs he could summon up from his memory. He also took us to his office building where, much to my brother's delight, he let him ride up and down in the *pater noster*, an elevator with no door; it did not stop at floors but slowly moved up and down in its shaft, and you had to enter and exit at just the right moment. The adventures of that visit have remained a happy memory. Our only subsequent visit occurred in February 1939, immediately before embarking in Bremerhaven for our emigration to America. It was a much more subdued mood in which we then found our Uncle Max. He was busy studying Spanish in preparation for their emigration to Colombia, South

America to join their son Werner, who had preceded them by more than ten years and already had a thriving business and a growing family. It was extremely fortunate for the Gordons that they had a son in Colombia, because Werner brought the entire family, parents and two sisters, out of Nazi Germany and into South America.

Aunt Else, of course, visited Breslau often, especially as long as Grandmother was alive. She clung with tremendous love to her entire family, but especially to her mother. Else was a warm and loving aunt, but a nervous type. She could never be happy in any situation for long. My mother used to say that when Else was in Breslau, she longed for Hamburg, and when in Hamburg, she couldn't wait to travel to Breslau. Her lifestyle was simple to an almost frightening degree. In her home, she would sit in the dark rather than waste electricity. She was extremely frugal and could not bear to accept even the smallest gift. Once when I bought her a very modest birthday present, she gave it back to me, insisting that she didn't need it. No amount of urging and cajoling could change her mind.

We had relatively little contact with our Gordon cousins, because they were much older and lived at some distance. Later on, however, Anni, the youngest, worked as a preschool teacher in the vicinity of Breslau and would visit often. She would bring her guitar and entertain us kids with songs and games. Werner never returned to Germany after his emigration, but once he sent his Colombian wife with two children to visit his parents and the whole extended family; it could not have been easy for his young wife who spoke not a word of German and had to look after her two young boys while meeting her husband's relatives, who, with the exception of Uncle Max, spoke only German. Much later, when we lived in Brooklyn, Werner came to visit. He was by then the father of four sons, but his first marriage had ended. Eventually he remarried and had a second family, two sons and a daughter

81

with his second wife. In 1987, he attended his aunt Edith's beatification in Cologne with his wife Maria and two sons, Heinz and Paul. He was by then a very sick man and died shortly thereafter. Werner had had a close connection with his aunt Edith; they exchanged many letters and Edith followed the events in her nephew's life with genuine loving concern.

As for my own parents, they lived under the same roof with Grandmother. We children never sensed any difficulties at the time, but we first got a whiff of such tensions in 1936, when Grandmother was suffering from stomach cancer. She was 86 years old at the time, and given her age and the state of medical knowledge at the time, surgery was apparently ruled out. Grandmother remained at home, surrounded by her devoted family who nursed and pampered her and tried to make her final months bearable. I believe the diagnosis was made some time early in the year, and when the time arrived for our customary vacation trip to the mountains, my mother had misgivings about leaving Grandmother. Father who could be very determined, not to say stubborn, was insistent, and so Mother agreed to travel to the *Altvater Mountains* with us, Father, my brother Ernst Ludwig and myself. The day before our scheduled departure, however, Grandmother took a turn for the worse, and Mother changed her mind and remained in Breslau. This turn of events gave rise to grave tensions between our parents, and our first few days in the mountains were darkened by Father's grouchy mood. After a furious exchange of letters, Mother appeared on the scene, but it was obvious even to us kids, that she had come under duress. The entire vacation period was spoiled for all of us by the gloomy atmosphere, the worry over Grandmother's condition and our sulking, resentful father. But the full extent of his resentment toward his mother-in-law did not really surface until decades later, in 1963, when he first read Edith Stein's manuscript of *Life in a Jewish Family* and relived every conflict, every argument, that had ever arisen between him and his mother-in-law, from the moment my parents announced their engagement in 1918.

I have referred elsewhere to a lengthy dissertation Father wrote to my brother and me, detailing his side of the story after reading Edith's. In it, he stresses that between himself and Auguste Stein a cordial relationship prevailed from their first encounter in 1909 to the moment when, ten years later, his status changed from that of Erna's friend to that of her fiancé. From then on he found his prospective mother-in-law hostile, critical and scheming.

I fear that, for this reason, my mother, too, became saddened after reading the book that her late sister had written and suffered as the pain and resentment of long-past conflicts were revived once more.

Much has been written about Auguste Stein's distress when first she learned about her youngest daughter's apostasy. I can only speak of that time based on my mother's account, for I was a newborn baby, when Tante Edith was baptized. Mother, as Edith's favorite sister, was entrusted not only with her secret but also with the unenviable task of informing her mother, as gently as possible. The scene described in the earliest biography of Edith Stein, by Sr. Teresia Renata [Posselt], in which Edith falls at the feet of her mother, exclaiming, "Mother, I am a Catholic!" is so melodramatic and totally inconsistent with Edith's character that it is surely apocryphal. I know for sure that my grandmother had received this information from my mother earlier. By the time my aunt took the next big step along her religious path, entering the Carmelite Order in 1933, I was old enough to be fully aware of the event. My brother and I, aged 10 and 11, were told by my parents that our aunt had become a Catholic years before and that she would now become a nun. I recall seeing Grandmother shedding silent tears. Her shoulders shook, but she made no sound. To me, a child of 11, it was a terrifying sight. The mere idea of a grownup unable to be in control of a situation was frightening to a child. And then the sight of our beloved grandmother in such distress was well-nigh unbearable. It must have been a combination of shame, grief and guilt that overwhelmed her thus. She surely had grieved in 1922, at the time of her daughter's conversion, and had asked herself how it could have happened and wherein she, her mother, might have failed. By 1933, yet another factor was added to the mix. It was the beginning of the anti-Jewish "Third Reich." Jews were being attacked viciously and a violent effort to drive them out of their homeland was under way. Under this threat, the Jewish community pulled together and became united. And just at that time, in her own family, her beloved child had chosen to become a cloistered nun. And finally, this was not just a convent, but a *Carmelite convent,* one of the strictest in existence. She might never see her daughter again. Whether Grandmother also asked herself, "Where did I go wrong? Could I have prevented this?" I cannot say. However, from my own experience as a mother, I can declare that when a child, even an adult "child" does something that appears wrong or misguided in a mother's eye, she will search for the cause within herself, at least in part. It seems to me more than likely that Edith's mother would have blamed herself for her failure to make Judaism sufficiently meaningful and valuable to her daughter to keep her from straying outside the fold.

As for the prospect that she might never again see Edith, it was somewhat mitigated by a glimmer of hope: A Carmelite monastery was about to be founded in a suburb of Breslau, and a possibility existed that Edith, after an initial time spent in Cologne, might be transferred there and thus be close enough to permit an occasional visit from her mother. Of course, it was far from certain that Auguste Stein could overcome her deep reluctance to set foot in such a place and actually pay a visit to a Carmelite monastery. As it turned out, my aunt never was transferred to the convent in Pawelwitz, [later Wendelborn] near Breslau, but remained in Cologne.

Sr. Amata Neyer here reveals an interesting, if disturbing twist concerning this subject:

> When the contemplated time for Edith Stein's transfer to Wendelborn approached, Sr.Elisabeth [Countess zu Stolberg-Stolberg,cousin of the prioress, Sr. Marianne, Countess Praschma] raised serious concerns about Edith Stein's admission to the Silesian Carmel and finally refused to approve this plan altogether. Her doubts about the advisability of this transfer were based upon the fact which had prompted Edith Stein to request this transfer, namely the geographic proximity of her family in Breslau. Although Sr. Elisabeth was far from harboring anti-Semitic prejudices, she anticipated difficulties for the recent foundation, if frequent visits from the Jewish family might conjure up suspicion on the part of neighbors with aggressively Nazi views and, through them, the attention of the fearsome Gauleiter [Head of an administrative district under National Socialism] . She kept repeating how much better the Carmel could help the Stein Family, if no non-Aryan Sister were living in the house. In fact, Sr. Elisabeth bought large supplies of lumber from the Stein lumber business for the construction of the new monastery in Wendelborn; that was a real help for the Stein firm which was by then in a totally depressed state. (My translation from the German.)[10]

In the nearly three years between her entry into Carmel in October, 1933 and my grandmother's death in September 1936, mother and daughter did not meet again. So deep was Auguste Stein's resentment that many months went by before she could bring herself to add even a short greeting to a letter which Edith's sisters were sending out to her.

Coincidentally with my aunt's entry into Carmel another change ocurred which my grandmother took very hard: We, my parents, my father's mother, my brother and I, moved out of the matriarchal home into the southern part of town. While we would not be more than a long trolley ride away from there, the daily contact with our extended family would be lacking. This made Grandmother sad, but it was an inevitable move. Mother would be taking over the gynecologic practice of one of her best friends, Dr. Lilli Berg-Platau, who was emigrating with her family to Palestine. Mother would be stepping into her thriving practice among Jewish patients in a predominantly upper middle class area, just as she was losing many of her non-Jewish patients who constituted the bulk of her practice in our old neighborhood. The large apartment which we were to occupy was designed as a combination living quarters and professional facility. Above the Berg-Platau domicile lived another physician's family, the Batzdorffs, a surgeon with his wife and two sons. We had not met that family, but in retrospect, our move proved providential, because eleven years later, and a continent away, I was to marry Alfred Batzdorff and start a life together with him which has by now lasted more than five decades. All this, of course, was unpredictable at the time, and I remember that we children strongly resisted this move, particularly because we were so aware of how hard Grandmother was taking it.

Grandmother lived for three more years after that. We visited her often, since our schools were not far from her home and we bicycled there every day. Besides, every Friday, we had a special reason for stopping at the family mansion: To pick up the fresh *challah,* the braided Shabbat bread which Aunt Rosa baked for the whole family. There were frequent visits back and forth, though Grandmother did not like to undertake long trolley trips any more. When she came, she would be dressed in her special black bonnet, tied with satin ribbons, which I only saw her wear to synagogue or for special outings.

When she fell ill, our visits to her bedside were frequent. When I first learned that she had been diagnosed with cancer, a word which was not even uttered aloud, I burst into tears. I remember Mother taking me aside and trying to reassure me with the words: "Now, don't feel so bad. It does not necessarily mean that Grandma can't get well." It was small comfort to me. Somehow I realized that things would go downhill, and I had better prepare myself for Grandmother's death.

Actually, it was not the first loss in our close family. In May 1934, my father's mother, who lived with us, had died in our apartment. She had suffered from heart disease for decades, and had survived many close calls. Her attacks of angina were severe and excruciatingly painful. That day, when she once again suffered such an attack, I heard her cries of pain and labored breathing, and I did not at first realize that the end had arrived for her.

When it was all over, Father would not let us children see her; he wanted us to remember her alive, as we had known her over the years. It is customary in Jewish mourning practice, that a *shomer* [someone who watches] remains with the body as long as it is in the house. The one who took over this important task was Grandmother Stein, who sat up all through the night reading psalms and keeping watch over my grandmother Dorothea Biberstein. The memory of her rendering that last service to a woman who was related to her by marriage and whom - I later found out - she did not especially like, returned to me after she, too, had died.

After Auguste Stein, the small but powerful matriarch of a large clan, died, there were subtle changes in the family dynamics. Although my aunts and my cousin stayed in the house, without Grandmother it wasn't the same. Besides the continuous encroachments of anti-Jewish legislation created much anxiety about the future. Somehow, the life of my grandmother and that of the large house in which so much family history had taken place, from the wedding of my parents to the births of four of my cousins, myself and, the following year, my brother , were intertwined. The eventual forced sale in 1939, which occurred after we had already left for America, was somehow an anti-climax. In her will, Grandmother bequeathed the house to her children, but they were able to hold on to it for only a short while.

That the house is now being dedicated to the cause of Catholic-Jewish dialogue and to building improved relations between Germans and Poles, is a comfort to me. In a way, it is a development which has been brought about despite the horrors of the Holocaust and of war, but also because of them. I shall not speculate what Auguste Stein or her daughter Edith might think of this, but for us, the survivors, it appears somehow appropriate.

CHAPTER 7

The Home of Auguste Stein, the Matriarch

By the time Edith finished *Gymnasium,* her mother's fortunes had improved and some time during the year 1910, she had purchased a handsome two-story house, large enough to accommodate most of her local family. By then Edith was nineteen years old, no longer a child. The house stood solid, conspicuous as a fairly elegant and affluent structure in a neighborhood of drab apartment houses, inhabited for the most part by working-class or lower middle class families. Its façade was adorned with stucco ornamentation, and in front of the building, a small flower garden extended to both sides of the house and was enclosed by a wrought-iron fence with a gate. Edith recalls the day of her *Abitur* (a final comprehensive examination at the end of high school), March 3, 1911, when she took a girlfriend, Julia Heimann, home with her during a break in the oral exams for some last-minute cramming and a bit of relaxation. Julia frankly expressed her surprise at finding such a fine home in so modest a neighborhood.

> She was impressed by the wide oak stairway and the huge living room to which I took her.[1]

This house was home to my grandmother and most of her children over the years. When we visited this house in June of 1995, I had not seen it since we left it in February 1939. I had been seventeen then, and now I was almost 74. Several members of the Edith Stein Society of Wroclaw accompanied us on this historic visit. To be honest, that is not the way I had envisioned this return to my childhood home. I had anticipated this event with mixed emotions. It might be traumatic, or at least upsetting. Such an experience, I thought, should be faced alone, or at most with close family members, but not with an entourage of strangers. At first the officers of the Edith Stein Society were reluctant to admit me to this place, because they knew that the house was in a state of disrepair and worried that it would make an unfavorable impression on me; however, after some hesitancy, they escorted me and members of my family to the front door. Someone put the large housekey in my hand.

The lock did not immediately yield. Once I stood in the dark, drab central hallway I so clearly remembered, it seemed quite natural to turn right, to the steps leading to the door of our erstwhile home, where we lived from birth until the fall of 1933. Suddenly I was a schoolgirl again, bounding up the steps with my leather satchel bouncing on my back, entering the front door. First came the living quarters (kitchen and dining-room) of my grandmother, her daughters Frieda and Rosa, and Frieda's daughter Erika. Also on the ground floor, my mother had her medical office and waiting room. Sometimes Mother would emerge from her office suite, white-coated and very professional-looking, for a quick hello. Here, awe-struck and mystified, I used to contemplate the various medical and surgical instruments which lay gleaming in a glass case. An elaborate circular staircase led to the upper floor which held a very elegant banquet room with adjoining "smoking room," both of vast proportions and with inlaid parquet floors, as well as the various bedrooms in which grandmother and the aunts slept. When Aunt Edith was vacationing in Breslau, she, too, inhabited one of the bedrooms on the upper floor.

An ample bathroom really served all the inhabitants of the house, as it had an efficient heater, a toilet and a bathtub, the only one in the house. I recall that when we were little, we used to be carried swiftly, wrapped securely in large bath sheets, from the unheated attic rooms where we lived, into the bathroom for our bath and shampoo, and afterwards returned at the same speed to our own quarters and to bed, so as to avoid catching cold during the transfer.

To the left was the home of Uncle Arno, his wife Martha and their four lively children, Wolfgang, Eva, Helmut and Lotte. They were our older cousins and, in spite of our age differences, our favorite playmates. In a letter of March 1, 1993, my cousin Wolf Stein recalls:

> In order to make an apartment, a kitchen and bathroom had to be installed...The bathtub and hot water heater were at one side of the kitchen, with a curtain, the toilet off the cellar steps, with the light switch outside, so the light could be shut off from the outside and a slow occupant forced out. [2]

Their living quarters must have been a fairly crowded space. I recall that the attic rooms in which my parents lived with us two children were also very modest. My brother's picturesque description may help to visualize the scenario:

> Our family lived just below the roof. At the time of my parents' marriage, the southern portion of the attic had been turned into a four-room apartment . The easternmost room with two windows was our parlor. Next door was the kitchen, a fairly large room, which included a sort of maid's room, divided off by a curtain. Behind the adjacent exterior windowless wall extended a long, dark corridor separating the eastern rooms from the two western ones. They were my parents' bedroom, and the children's room. On the north side of the attic, there were two attic rooms, chiefly for the purpose of drying laundry and storing suitcases and other household goods that were not in regular use. Within the westernmost attic space, behind a wooden partition, was the toilet. Even though I can't remember such details today, it appears to me in retrospect that using the toilet in winter

91

> must have been a Spartan undertaking, since, of course, these lofts were not heated. The other rooms had tile stoves, while the lower floors already had central steam heat...[3]

What my brother refrains from telling is that my parents had to battle rats in the unfinished attic in the early days. My mother would frequently retell with horror how she dreaded a visit to the toilet during the night, because an encounter with a furtive rodent was something she found terrifying. In fact, Father would be summoned to dispatch the hateful critter with his shotgun. Fortunately all this happened before my brother and I were born.

At the time of my parents' marriage, in December 1920, there was a severe housing shortage, due to the effects of the First World War and the poverty into which it had plunged the country. It was thus more by necessity than by choice that my parents settled there. Grandmother Stein, of course, was happy about that, because she really preferred to have all her "chicks" under one roof, or at least as many as possible. We inhabited this attic apartment from the time my parents married until 1928, when a population shift took place in the house . At that time, Uncle Arno, Aunt Martha and their four children moved out, and Father's mother, Grandmother Biberstein, moved in with us. We transferred to rooms on the second floor, while Grandma Stein and her daughters and granddaughter occupied the west side of the ground floor which Arno Stein and family had vacated.

When we lived there, grapevines trailed up the walls of the house, and I can remember reaching out from our living-room window and plucking sour grapes. Among my fondest memories of this house are the hours we spent in play with our cousins in the backyard, where we had various pieces of gymnastic and play equipment, a set of parallel bars, a horizontal bar, a sandbox and the inevitable carpet beating rack which was present in every self-respecting German backyard in those days. In one corner there was also a large elderberry bush, from which one summer we helped ourselves to vast quantities of berries, with disastrous results to our digestive systems which still remain unpleasantly in my memory.

On Saturday afternoons about four o'clock, a large black automobile, I think it was a Horch, would drive up in front of the house, and from its padded ample interior would emerge my grandmother's sisters, Malchen Pick, Selma Horowitz and Clara Courant. Malchen had five daughters and two sons. Hans Horowitz, Aunt Selma's son, was the chauffeur, who drove the three sisters to their weekly afternoon Kaffeklatsch with their older sister Gustel. My grandmother held a certain position, not just of seniority, but also of prestige and respectability, perhaps because of her status as a successful businesswoman or because of her standing in the family. Grandmother had fourteen siblings. These four sisters were the only ones who lived in Breslau, while the youngest sister Emma lived in Berlin as did three brothers. Tante Selma was short and round and slightly stooped over. She was the mother of six sons, of whom five lived to adulthood. She had been a widow since 1917. Hans was the only one of her sons who lived in town. Malchen, whose full name was Amalie, but no one ever called her that, had borne five daughters and two sons. Her husband Julius had lost his eyesight before we knew him and he died while we were young children. It was perhaps the first death in the family that I recall. Tante Clara was a tall, gaunt woman with a hooked nose. She was very good-natured and liked to laugh. She was a favorite with us children. I believe that none of the sisters had the intelligence of my grandmother, but they all looked up to her and deferred to her. All four sisters were always dressed in black.

Hans Horowitz, an attorney, was one of a set of twins, (Franz being the other one) and one of my mother's erstwhile cavaliers who, perhaps still carried a torch for her. At the time I never wondered what Hans was doing in this circle of four women of his mother's generation, but he probably enjoyed Aunt

93

Rosa's excellent cakes and strong coffee, which invariably were served on these occasions.

Decades later, my brother Ernst Ludwig Biberstein was asked to write his recollections about this house for the benefit of the Edith Stein Society of Wroclaw, who now own this building. His description of the "huge living room" may shed additional light on the splendor of this impressive interior:

> On the south side of the first floor were the two palatial rooms in the house, a thirty-three feet long "Saal" with four huge windows and an adjoining somewhat smaller, though still ample "smoking room". Some particulars about these rooms I still remember. The "Saal" had a parquet floor of inlaid wood in various colors in a large rhomboid pattern. In the southeastern corner of the "Saal" stood my mother's Bechstein grand piano, which in retrospect appeared of the size of a jet runway, and which could not be accommodated in our little attic apartment. The only piece of furniture that could perhaps equal this piece of furniture in size and weight, was the monumental dining table, a monster with elaborately turned legs of vast dimensions. On solemn occasions this table could be expanded...to amazing length, by means of countless table inserts, so as to take up almost all the space in the large room. According to tradition, this occurred at my parents' wedding feast and, in my own memory, on grandmother Stein's eightieth birthday. Yet another piece of furniture which I clearly remember was Aunt Edith's black laquered desk with the rather uncomfortable desk chair... An almost murderous tale was told about Mr. Schmidt, the watchmaker across the street, who one night fired his pistol in the air in order to coax a few noisy late-night strollers to move on. The shot apparently went up diagonally across the street through the window above Aunt Edith's desk and embedded itself in the beautiful ceiling. No one was hurt in our house, since the Stein family was used to retiring early, and so no one noticed what had happened until the next morning.[4]

As for occasions when the large dining table was expanded to its full length, let us not forget the Seder night, the first night of Passover, when the extended family gathered to observe the elaborate ceremonial dinner, with Father reciting the story of Exodus in Hebrew, and all of us joining in the singing of the many familiar tunes and everyone filling up on the traditional foods, such as hard-cooked eggs with salt water, a reminder of the tears of our enslaved ancestors in Egypt, and the delicious apple and nut concoction called *haroset,* which was eaten to recall the mortar which our forebears used in the making of the bricks they were forced to produce.

Contrary to our own detailed recollections, based on personal memory and authenticated stories told by the older generation, all of them one-time residents of this house, descriptions by "outsiders" [who have never seen these premises] are more fanciful and do not always reflect the facts.

Unfortunately it was the very first biography of Edith Stein that first contained these misleading statements and continues to give its readers an erroneous impression of what life in Grandmother's home was like. Since I lived in the same house and was able to look around daily until the age of twelve, I can assure you that it contained no "engravings illustrating scenes from the history of Israel nor beautiful carving on cupboards and chests displaying exclusively biblical motifs" and thus no one who entered this house would have had a "sense of having been carried back into the Old Testament " or of "being in the house of a devout rabbi."[5] Such décor would have been highly uncommon and not at all compatible with the biblical injunction against "graven images." In her eagerness to picture my grandmother's home life as devoutly Jewish, Sr. Teresia Renata further states that "grace was said in Hebrew, and every appropriate ceremonial prescription of the Talmud was precisely carried out".[6]

Now my mother, upon reading this, consistently and vehemently denied that Hebrew prayers were spoken at mealtime; in fact she would remark that her mother was "much too busy" to find time for prayers, before or after meals. And as for the laws of the Talmud, Grandmother would have had no knowledge of these. It is true that she followed Jewish tradition as she had learned it from her parents and experienced it in her parental home, but neither she nor her children would have been aware of Talmudic lore. My mother, during her lifetime, made every effort to correct these statements, but to

95

no avail; nor did later editions of the biography bring corrections of any kind. We, the family of Edith Stein, got the impression that such manifestations of poetic license might have been directed by a purpose, namely that of depicting an atmosphere of such oppressive orthodoxy as to alienate a sensitive nature such as Edith's from her faith and to propel her toward Christianity. I cannot speculate as to what prompted the author to engage in such flights of fancy. Knowing Edith's meticulous respect for truth, I cannot believe that such tales originated with her. I rather suspect that the author's desire to create a fascinating story may have led her to embellish it a bit. She could hardly foresee that her imaginative tales would give rise to an entire trend of speculation concerning the course of Edith Stein's spiritual development.

Getting back to the mundane matter of the house purchase, none of the surviving grandchildren know how much my grandmother paid for it. The house was still within easy walking distance of grandmother's lumberyard, and she walked to and from work daily, rain or shine, until well into her eighties. This capacious house was home to grandmother Auguste, her children Frieda, Rosa, Erna and Edith, her granddaughter Erika, Frieda's only child, and my uncle Arno with his wife and four children. For a time there also lived in this house my grandmother's younger sister Mika, who was paralyzed and bedridden after a severe stroke and who lingered on for about two years, and their much younger sister Clara, who was also single and nursed Mika devotedly and patiently during her final illness.

There were several "population shifts" over the years; the most radical one occurred in 1928, when Uncle Arno and family moved to another location and my paternal grandmother Dorothea Biberstein moved in. She was at that time severely ill with heart disease, and my father considered it imperative that she give up her apartment and live with us.

Since this house has had a remarkable existence and survived war and devastation, I want to give a short history of what I know about it from the time Grandmother acquired it until the present.

This house was originally built as a "villa" for a brewer by the name of A. Sindermann on a plot of land known as "Vier Türme" [Four Towers][7] After my grandmother's death in September 1936, it remained the home of my aunts Frieda and Rosa while a part of the house was rented out to various tenants. In 1939, due to new restrictive legislation, Jews were no longer permitted to own real estate, and the house had to be sold to an "Aryan." Clearly, under these circumstances, prospective buyers knew of the bind in which the seller found himself, and this depressed the real estate prices of Jewish-owned property. A builder by the name of Oskar Jandel bought it for 20,000 marks (the equivalent of about $8,000 at that time).[8]

By then, the remaining family members were actively pursuing their emigration. Rosa had already left for Belgium, where a Catholic home was being established and where she was to serve as housekeeper, bringing a large portion of household goods and furniture along to help furnish the new establishment. My cousin Erika Tworoger, daughter of aunt Frieda, had left for what was then Palestine to study nursing at Shaarei Tsedek hospital in Jerusalem, leaving only Frieda, who moved into an apartment with several other women. Subsequently Jews were forced to move into ever more crowded quarters and finally deported eastward to Theresienstadt, where most of them either died of starvation or infectious diseases or were deported to Auschwitz and gassed.

My brother, ends his nostalgic essay about Grandmother's house thus:

> In the last spring of her life, my grandmother often sat in
> the almost gardenlike part of the backyard in a deckchair.
> Later she spent several months in her room on the upper

floor, with windows facing that yard and perhaps wafting some of the jasmine scent up to her when she was bedfast and did not have much longer to live. She died in this room in this house which she had acquired a generation earlier for her family and which represented a sort of family castle, a focal point and a symbol even long after all who had ever been connected with it had been scattered in all directions.[9]

In the last months of World War II, seventy percent of the buildings in Breslau were destroyed. The house on 38 Michaelisstrasse still stood at war's end. Under the Communist rule, the house became state property, but in 1951 Odra-Film, a motion picture enterprise acquired it.[10] The Edith Stein Society of Wroclaw [Towarzystwo im. Edyty Stein] initiated efforts to buy this property in order to create a center for disseminating knowledge of the life and work of Edith Stein, a place for Polish-German as well as Christian-Jewish dialogue and guest rooms for overnight stays. Toward that end, the Edith Stein Society began a campaign for funds to acquire and restore this house. They managed to have it declared a public monument and installed a plaque in Polish, German and Hebrew as a reminder that Blessed Edith Stein lived here. The plaque is in the same spot where, in my youth, Mother's doctor's shingle used to hang next to the bell by which she could be summoned at night. The city of Wroclaw was able to arrange a real estate swap by which the firm Odra-Film accepted a city-owned piece of land in the downtown area in exchange for the house which the Edith Stein Society so ardently wanted to obtain. The Society for German-Polish Cooperation paid for the acquisition of the property from the city, while donated funds are being used to cover the cost of restoration. Grandmother had intended to leave this home to her children as an inheritance and focal point for the family. At her death she could not fully foresee the scattering of her loved ones and the tragedy that was to befall them. We, their offspring, find a certain comfort in the knowledge that it will now be dedicated to a worthy cause, that of better relations among people of different faiths and nationalities.

We visited this house in June 1995, when restoration work had not yet begun, and again in June 1997, when the workers were milling about, and an elevator shaft had been installed. The elevator cab was sitting in the backyard, where we, Auguste Stein's grandchildren, used to swing on the parallel bars and dangle from the horizontal bar or dig in the sandbox. As kids we used to run up and down the oaken circular staircase or slide on the banisters, but during our 1995 visit just ascending it was clearly a risky enterprise and not everyone in our party was willing to attempt it.

The restoration aims to reproduce this house as faithfully as possible, although an additional floor is being added to accommodate office space and overnight quarters for visitors. The blue plexiglas enclosure enveloping this addition stands in peculiar contrast to the somber grey exterior of the historical edifice which we once called home.

At our 1995 visit, the officers of the Society were confident that by the World Eucharistic Congress scheduled for May 1997, the house would be ready for use and for show. However, this was not possible. The work of restoration is proving to be far more extensive and expensive than originally contemplated, and it may be another few years before the long-awaited solemn dedication can take place.

I had prepared myself for a painful experience revisiting this scene of my youth, but I was surprised. This empty shell from which all past life had long fled, had no message for me any more. After returning home, I wrote a poem reflecting my reaction to this encounter:

HOME—56 YEARS LATER

The key turns, reluctant
To open the familiar door—
Inside yawns emptiness,
Grey, sooty walls,
Creaking banisters crawl
Alongside curving stairs.

Did nimble feet
Hop, skip here,
Taking those stairs
Two at a time
In the long ago,
In the time before time?

Family life,
Voices, laughter,
Song, piano chords,
Where have they gone?
Even the ghosts
Shun these stark interiors.
Can these bones live?
Can these walls speak?
They do not speak to me.
Memories have fled,
They don't cling to these walls.
Perhaps when we left,
They followed us
Into foreign lands,
To wrap us velvetlike,
Softly.

This is the house
That has tales to tell,
Stories to share,
But not with me.

I must look now
Towards other shores
Where the future lives,
Where children grow,
Where young feet skip
Down other steps.
I must leave this place alone,
Once and for all.
This house,
Far older than I,
Has new lives to live.
As for my memories,
They live in me.

When Aunt Edith had completed her first year of university studies in Breslau, she realized that the focus of her intellectual inquiry had changed. She would go to Göttingen to study with the originator of phenomenology, Edmund Husserl, who, she felt, was the leading light in philosophy at the time.

Thus, Edith Stein hardly ever lived in what is now known as "the Edith Stein house", though she visited it whenever she spent her vacations in Breslau.

A bit of misinformation has crept into some writings by subsequent authors indicating that this house was acquired in 1903 and thus that Edith "grew up in this home." The error is traceable to the fact that the first edition of Edith Stein's autobiographical account *Aus dem Leben einer jüdischen Familie,* Herder, 1965, was an abridged edition, and one of these abridgments resulted in an unfortunate ambiguity.[11] In fact, while this was Edith's home from 1910 until her entry into Carmel, she mostly lived elsewhere and only returned for vacations or occasionally, as during World War I, for a more extended stay.

CHAPTER 8

Pioneers at the University of Breslau

For me, one aspect of life in our family has always stood out, the tremendous respect for education. I remember clearly my father's frequently repeated dictum: "They can take your money and possessions. But what is in your head, nobody can take away from you." Likewise, in Grandmother Stein's family, education was greatly valued. Therefore, it must have been a great sorrow to her that economic hardships prevented her from giving her older children the education for which they may have been qualified. Only the two youngest ones got to study at the university. The other remarkable fact is that in our family the thought never occurred to anyone that girls need not be educated. My mother began her university studies in 1909, just one year after women were first admitted to academic education in Prussia.

Father used to tell us how he met Mother. It was while they were both registering for their first semester at the university, on April 30, 1909. One criterion for Father in the selection of a life companion was that she had to be at least five years younger than he. When he looked over Erna Stein's shoulder, therefore, and saw that she was but two months younger than he, he immediately dismissed her as a candidate for marriage but took note of her name for future reference, just in case. He foolishly entertained the notion that women students were all ugly and wore glasses. One look at this attractive young woman convinced him to abandon his prejudices. And how grateful we are that he acknowledged his error!

Here is Edith Stein's portrait of Hans Biberstein, when she first met him:

> On the tennis court I met the one who was soon to supplant me at my sister's side, however not in such a way as to result in a real separation for us. This was totally unnecessary since the two of us, Hans Biberstein and I, hit it off at once. Immediately as he took his place opposite me on the tennis court, I liked him very much. The white tennis outfit admirably set off his tanned face and his shining black hair, both of which were singularly contrasted by sparkling light eyes. He was slim, short, and muscular; and he, himself, bounced from one end of he court to the other as lightly as a rubber ball.[1]

She recalls that before her *Abitur* (a final comprehensive examination at the conclusion of High School), he studied history with her. "Once, sometime later, Hans admitted to my sister that she would have had some cause to be jealous of me at that particular time." Judging by several passages in her autobiography and by remarks Father made to us in later years, the suspicion that they were attracted to each other cannot be denied. Father was a good dancer, and Edith recalls the various occasions when they danced together, from their student days on through the day of my parents' wedding.

> "...we would seat Erna at the piano and dance while she played. One could not have wished for a better partner than Hans; I used to say that when one danced with him one forgave him every last fault. The two of us fully appreciated dancing for its own sake. My sister cared for it less than we; and only with my brother-in-law did she dance well and with pleasure.[2]

I find a bitter-sweet tone in Edith's nostalgic recollection of my parents' wedding celebration:

At that time my health was very poor, probably as a result of the emotional [or spiritual?][3] conflicts I then endured in complete secrecy and without any human support...By evening, I was fine again. At first I did not join in the dancing. But when it had grown late and I was standing near the grand piano beside Hans, they suddenly began to play an old, well-known, lively number. "Isn't that a fast-step?" I asked. That was a dance which had become popular during our student years, and I had learned it from Hans. "Yes," he said, "Would you care to dance? I did not dare ask you earlier since you hadn't been feeling well." We began and did not stop until the whole exuberant number was over. As Hans was about to lead me to a seat, the music for a slow waltz began. "Well," he said, "now we have to show people we also know how to dance elegantly"; and we finished the entire waltz. I have never again really danced since then.[4]

Hans and Edith shared a lifelong interest in history and politics, and their letters throughout the years reflect their concern with these subjects. Somewhere in her writings, Edith mentioned that, while she was perhaps initially smitten with this attractive young man, she did not allow this feeling to prevail, because she was aware of how Erna felt about him. I believe that this was true and I know that Edith Stein remained a close friend of Hans's, quite apart from her relationship as a sister-in-law.

I have always considered myself lucky to have grown up in a family where the equality of the sexes was an established tradition. Both my parents had been in the forefront of the battle for women's rights. No father could have been more ambitious on behalf of a daughter than my own. Both he and my mother had grown up in fatherless households where the mother was head of the household and had to be both mother and father to her children besides earning the wherewithal to support her family. The idea that a woman's place is in the home never had a chance to take hold. It was rather more like the current motto, "A woman's place is anywhere she wants [or needs] to be."

And yet, one had to be pragmatic. Not all doors stood wide open to women, and especially Jewish women. Edith relates in her book that she and her sister Erna visited their uncle David, a pharmacist in Chemnitz, right after Erna's *Abitur*.

Aside from being a cordial host and trying to give the two young girls a good time, Uncle David also exhorted them about planning their future. He urged them to study medicine. Edith, who did not have to make that decision for another two years, was determined not to let anyone influence her in her career choice, but Erna, upon her return home, announced to her mother that she would study medicine.[5]

Edith, who stuck to her guns, dedicating herself to the study of philosophy and later hoping for a professorship at a university, was to find herself facing a wall of anti-Semitic and antifeminist prejudice and had to settle for a teaching position at a Catholic institution in Münster, the next best thing to a bona fide academic appointment.

We often heard my mother say in later years that she came to appreciate Uncle David's advice, although at the time she would have preferred to study modern languages and become a teacher. Subsequently she realized that as a doctor, she had the opportunity to practice a free profession and be independent of public bureaucratic institutions which were not eager to offer employment to Jews or to women.

The position of women students at the University of Breslau was far from clarified. Edith reports, rather amusingly, how the women fit into the celebration of the one hundredth anniversary of the *Schlesische Friedrich-Wilhelm-Universität:*

> I truly considered the university my "alma mater" and so delighted in taking part in her jubilee celebration. Naturally we attended the major festivity in the Aula, the great hall; but we had some misgivings about joining in the student festival...The Women's Student Union held many discussions; we had received reports from the Berlin University that at the jubilee celebration there the previous year some unpleasant incidents had occurred. For that reason we initially declined to attend. Thereupon we received a second invitation from "His Magnificence," the president of the university: he would be deeply saddened were the women students to absent themselves from the event; he would have some of the professors' wives assigned to our tables to prevent unpleasant incidents. So we agreed

105

after all, but, considering it ridiculous, we declined his offer to provide "mothering." We decided we would stay until the actual merriment, the "Fidelitas," would begin, and then withdraw quietly at that point. This worked very well. Naturally, the attention of the "old boys" [the alumni]...was drawn to the table at which the girls, all in white dresses, were seated; after all, there had been nothing like that "in their time."[6]

Among my mother's old documents there are printed report forms certifying that my mother had passed various required courses. The male pronouns on these forms had to be hand-corrected in ink for use with female students.

The friends my parents and Edith made during their student years remained lifelong friends, and during our childhood my brother and I were regaled with anecdotes of their adventures during those comparatively carefree years. Erna and Edith, a year apart but growing up almost like twins, continued this closeness by sharing many friends, causes, and ideals. Somehow they drew other congenial students like a magnet, people who were thoughtful, intelligent, but who also had a sense of humor and found enjoyment in outdoor activities. They played tennis, hiked and climbed mountains. Most were not affluent and lived frugally. All were academically ambitious and politically aware. They adopted causes such as women's suffrage and various social legislation. Though they were patriotic Germans, they shied away from uncritical or fanatic nationalism, partly because such thinking often went hand in hand with anti-Semitism, and most of their friends were Jewish.

Edith sketches loving portraits of these people and includes in the circle also their parents.

In the class between ours there were two inseparable friends, Lilli Platau and Rose Guttmann...Only when Lilli began to study medicine and so shared the same lectures and lab courses, did Erna get to know them better. Soon Erna and Lilli formed close ties. Rose was taking mathematics and natural sciences; and when I came to the university, we found ourselves attending philosophy and psychology lectures together. Soon we, too, were bosom friends; and the two pairs then fused to form an indivisible four-leaf clover. As he was inseparable from Erna, Hans was grafted on like some fifth leaf. But in no way was it a matter of our tolerating him merely for her sake, rather each one of us had a bond with him, not only of sincere friendship but of mutual intellectual interests as well.[7]

Summer vacations in the Riesengebirge in 1911 and near Reinerz the following year are recalled nostalgically in Edith's book, but they also were part of the tradition in our own family and formed a chain of memories which were told and retold by our parents. We were always impressed by the relative freedom with which they were allowed to travel. No one appeared to care what "people might say" about male and female friends going on overnight hikes together, rooming in mountain inns, accommodating themselves to whatever rooms or dubious alcoves were available. While close friendship united Edith with everyone, she did not hesitate to criticize the foibles and weaknesses in her circle of companions. Hans and his mother come in for particularly acerbic criticism, and it was with a sense of shock that I remember first reading these passages. Edith's critique of my father and grandmother ranges from ridicule to sharp censure:

> ...When we first met him, we were amazed to learn that he was not allowed to go rowing with us. It had been forbidden him, once and for all, as too dangerous[8]

> ...son and mother not only criticized their relatives but ...also made fun of their weaknesses in front of us and of more distant acquaintances. But, taking this outspokenness as a true indication of their attitude would have been a mistake, since it had become so habitual with them to amuse themselves at the expense of others that hardly anyone among their relatives and acquaintances was safe from their sharp tongues. In the long run, under these circumstances, relations with them were liable to become strained. Besides, both were excessively sensitive and suspected that an intent to offend lurked behind the most harmless remark made to them; they were likely to take offense instantaneously and obviously. My good mother, who always freely spoke her mind and who could never get accustomed to weighing her words scrupulously, unwittingly conjured up a storm on countless occasions.[9]

107

She describes him as spoiled and comments that his mother would brag about his accomplishments to everyone. From my mother I learned that these portrayals, coming as they did some fifty years later, caused much grief to both my parents at first reading, particularly since Father reacted very emotionally, allowing it to revive long-buried conflicts with people who were long dead. He resented the fact that what he perceived as gross misrepresentations were not only published for all to see but could no longer be debated with Edith. He did the only thing open to him and wrote a sharp and detailed response to her allegations, for my brother and myself, to "set the record straight." While I do not want to accuse Edith of deliberate distortion of facts, I do detect in her story a one-sided point of view, in which she somewhat uncritically takes the side of her mother, disregarding some very significant factors, particularly the grave disability of my paternal grandmother. In the words of Hans Biberstein:

> ...Everyone in this circle, not just Mother (Erna) and her family... knew that I would never leave my mother on her own, not even in case I married. My clearly stated reason was that my mother suffered from a severe heart disease ever since a bout with rheumatic fever in the winter of 1904... I was able to talk about this determination of mine with all our friends without creating the impression that it was intended to discourage girls who had marriage on their minds or prospective mothers-in-law with a "readily honed" blessing, since I had the admittedly foolish idea that a match with any of these young women was out of the question because we were all of the same age... With the outbreak of war in 1914, Mother and I decided to marry,...if I survived the war.[10]

Thus, my father's close relationship to his mother must be understood, keeping in mind that he felt responsible for caring for his mother in her illness. He felt a great debt of thanks to her for having raised him alone, since his father had died when Hans was 1 1/2 years old.

Just one week after his safe return from military service as a medical doctor, on December 26, 1918, my father, true to his plan, called upon his future mother-in-law to ask for Erna's hand in marriage "for all concerned, even those who knew us only slightly...a mere formality". Everyone took it for granted that Hans and Erna would marry. However, from this moment on, relations between him and his mother-in-law changed radically. My father submits that Grandmother Stein pursued a systematic policy to subvert their efforts of finding an apartment in the southern part of Breslau, an area with a large Jewish population, where Erna would have excellent prospects of establishing a lucrative practice as the first Jewish gynecologist in town. The end of the war was a time of extreme housing shortage and it was their plan to offer my paternal grandmother's apartment in exchange for a larger one in the same area. Father, however, alleges that Auguste Stein was determined to have her daughter Erna establish her practice in her home on Michaelisstrasse, a working class neighborhood with a minimal Jewish population, and to force the young couple to live at that address. Coincidentally this made Father's plan of keeping his mother with them impossible, since there was no room for her in the small attic apartment which ultimately became my parents' first dwelling after their marriage.

Most painful for my father was the insinuation on the part of Edith that the presence of his mother in their household would have made my mother's existence wretchedly unhappy. Still, throughout his lengthy commentary, he asserts his love and respect for his sister-in-law Edith, her honesty and her absolute trustworthiness. In his introduction he says:

> Edith played a very significant role [in our circle of friends] not just as Mother's sister, but she received next to her my complete confidence, almost without limits.[11]

He acknowledges with warmth her role as a peacemaker and go-between in disputes between him and his mother-in-law and only expresses bewilderment at the difference between her role then and her way of presenting the story in her book.

Not every one of Edith's relatives had the opportunity to comment on what had been said about him or her. Most were no longer around. Of the nephews and nieces who read the account of their parents in this chronicle, several resorted to similar means of taking a stand or correcting false impressions that might result from the way their parents' story was told. In the following chapters, some of these remarks are cited. They vary from brief spoken remarks in conversation with me to detailed essays and letters written in response to Edith Stein's presentation.

CHAPTER 9

Dear Göttingen!

Dear Göttingen! I do believe only someone who studied here
between 1905 and 1914, the short flowering of the Göttingen
School of Phenomenology, can appreciate all that resonates
in that name.

I was twenty-one years old and looked forward full of
expectation to all that lay ahead.[1]

The aspect of romance that clung to Edith Stein's move to a
university away from home probably was based on a
combination of following the seductive call to study with a
scholar of great renown, Edmund Husserl, the founder of
phenomenology, and the heady awareness that this would be
the first time Edith left her parental home to venture on an
entirely independent path of her own. Remarkably, her mother
put no obstacle in her way, even though she certainly could
not fully appreciate why Edith needed to embark on this
adventure. After all, Erna was content to pursue her medical
studies at the University of Breslau, living under her mother's
roof. And yet their mother said, "If you need to go there to
study, I certainly won't bar your way." She was, however,
unaccountably sad, "much sadder than a short absence for a
summer's semester warranted."[2] In retrospect, it makes one
wonder whether my grandmother had a foreboding that this

111

step would lead her daughter away from the path which she had envisioned for her. For that is surely what turned out to be true.

Edith had first been made aware of Husserl by Dr. Georg Moskiewicz, an older fellow-student at the University of Breslau. He steered her toward Husserl's *Logical Investigations*. He had spent a semester as a student of Husserl in Göttingen and longed to return there. "In Göttingen, " he told her, "all you do is philosophize, day and night, at meals, in the street, everywhere. All you talk about is 'phenomena.'" Even more beguiling for Edith would have been the fact that one of Husserl's students was a young woman, Hedwig Martius, who had just received a prize in philosophy. One final argument, which may have reconciled Mother Auguste to this idea was the fact that Richard Courant, Edith's cousin, had just settled in Göttingen with his wife Nellie. Thus Edith would not be entirely without family in a strange city. Edith also had persuaded her friend Rose Guttmann to join her for this summer semester in Göttingen. It was one thing to chart new paths,but it would be reassuring to take a bit of home with her, just one friend to share in this enterprise.

Edith first visited her sister Else and family in Hamburg. Max Gordon, her brother-in-law was concerned about letting her go off into the world all alone and attempted to talk her into spending at least the first night at the Courants, but Edith refused. Richard and Nellie had found lodgings for her, and she was eager to go there straightaway and settle in. On April 17, she left Hamburg so as to arrive in Göttingen before the semester officially began. As she watched the passing countryside from the window of a speeding train, she must have been dreaming of all the new impressions, new friends, new adventures waiting for her in the small university town of Göttingen.

Filled with joyous anticipation, Edith checked into her lodgings, where the young landlady greeted her with a smile.

Later, she admitted her own pleased surprise at my appearance. She had never had any women students in her home before and thought they would all be old and ugly. Nearly every household in Göttingen rented rooms to students. On principle, many landladies refused women boarders. Some had moral prejudices. Others feared their kitchens would be in demand too frequently for washing, ironing, or cooking.[3]

Characteristically, Edith immediately set out on an exploratory walk around the city and found much to her liking. Unlike Breslau, Göttingen was solely a university town. The university and the students gave it its flavor and unique character. With about 30, 000 inhabitants, it was much smaller than Breslau and had no public transportation. The sweet scent of linden trees intoxicated her and the presence of many memorial plaques affixed to the houses in which in times past famous residents of Göttingen had lived[4] conveyed a sense of history to the impressionable newcomer. For there were such eminent names as the Brothers Grimm, the physicists Gauss and Weber, and the poet Heinrich Heine.

Life in Göttingen wasn't all work and no play for Edith and Rose. They took full advantage of the beautiful surroundings and made many walking tours extending over several days. Later when my mother Erna visited, she, too, was treated to these outings and in later years remembered them in an essay:

After our medical State Board Examinations, my friend, who later became my husband, and I decided to visit Edith and Rose in Göttingen. We spent an unforgettable time, with delightful excursions and hours of fun in which she did her utmost to show us her beloved Göttingen and its attractive environs at their best. Following that visit, we took a hike through the very beautiful Harz mountains.[5]

It makes me glad to see that my aunt's first words about Göttingen are devoted to picturing its charms, its sounds and smells and the charm of its environs, and only then does she turn to "the essential topic—the one which had led me to Göttingen: phenomenology and the phenomenologists." For serious scholars—and Edith Stein was surely one of them—that is the most important matter; but it is reassuring for me to discover that, as a girl of twenty-one, experiencing her first heady taste of freedom, she was capable of having fun with her friends and discovering that there was a world beyond books and desks and cramming for exams.

She soon reports, however, that she wasted no time before paying a call to the Reinachs, for she had been told that Adolf Reinach was the key person to contact; he was Husserl's right hand and provided the necessary liaison between "the master" and his students. Their first meeting boded well for the future, for Reinach received her with an open friendliness; he was not the least bit pompous or condescending toward this newcomer, and Edith gained courage to venture onto new territory and meet new challenges. Reinach even accepted her for his "advanced exercises". As for the eminent Professor Husserl, she would meet him later.

For a New Year's party the year preceding Edith's move to Göttingen, her friends wrote for her this prophetic ditty,

> Many a maiden dreams of "busserl"[kisses],
> Edith, though, of naught but Husserl,
> In Göttingen she soon will see
> Husserl as real as real can be.[6]

> Neither striking nor overwhelming, his external appearance was rather of an elegant professorial type. His height was average; his bearing, dignified; his head, handsome and impressive. His speech at once betrayed his Austrian birth; he came from Moravia and had studied in Vienna. His serene amiability also had something of old Vienna about it. He had just completed his fifty-fourth year.[7]

Edmund Husserl was not a full professor, but merely an "extraordinary professor" (comparable to an Assistant Professor in American parlance), and his status at the university was that of an outsider. His innovative thinking was viewed with suspicion by his more conservative colleagues,

> Husserl's new tone attracted some students in Göttingen, to be sure. But whoever cared about pursuing a career for himself or wanted to complete his doctorate without a lot of

Salomon Courant,
grandfather of Edith Stein

Adelheid Courant,
grandmother of Edith Stein

Siegfried Stein (tallest in photo) with his siblings, c. 1861

Edith Stein's family. Back row, left to right: Arno (1879-1948), Else (1876-1956), Siegfried (1843-1893), Elfriede (1881-1942), Paul (1872-1943): front row, left to right: Rosa (1883-1942), Auguste (nee Courant, 1849-1936), Edith (1891-1942), Erna (1890-1978). Of the seven children, four fell victim to the Nazi holocaust — Paul, Elfriede, Rosa and Edith.

Auguste Stein in her vegetable garden

Ice Skating on the "Waschteich"

Erna and Edith c. 1899-1900,
Edith on right

Edith with sister Erna and ne
Gerhard, c. 1905, Edith on

Edith Stein as a teenager in Hamburg with her
eldest sister Else and her two children

Edith Stein as a student,
c. 1913-1914 in Göttingen

Edith Stein, 1926

Home of Auguste Stein, nee Courant, Michaelis St. 38, Wroclaw (formerly Breslau). In the windows on the upper floor, Susanne (author of this book), Ernst Ludwig Biberstein (niece and nephew of Edith Stein) with their paternal grandmother, Dorothea Biberstein. At the next window to the right, Dr. Erna Biberstein, nee Stein, sister of Edith.

Susanne and Ernst Ludwig at living room window c. 1930

1938 passport photo of Edith Stein,
taken before she left for Holland

Auguste Stein c. 1936

Rosa Stein in late 1930s

Edith Stein with her older sister Rosa, 1942, shortly before both were deported to Auschwitz

Dr. Hans Biberstein, c. 1960

Dr. Erna Biberstein c. 1960

After the beatification ceremony. From left to right: Alfred Batzdorff, Susanne
Batzdorff, Bernhard Rosenmoller (whose family were close to Edith Stein),
Pope John Paul II, Cardinal Hoffner and Mr. Solzbacher, an aide to the cardinal.

complications, had better stick to the full professors the ones with power, since they could not expect much from the luckless outsider Husserl.[8]

Husserl was an original thinker and a learned man, but he was not, from the testimony of his erstwhile students, a spellbinding lecturer. "Terribly boring," said Ernst Rappeport, and Richard Courant called his lectures " a soporific." Adolf Reinach, by contrast, knew how to make the material clear and comprehensible to the novices, and it was "not a matter of lecturing and learning, but rather of searching together under the direction of a reliable and knowledgeable guide".[9] Thus these phenomenology students felt themselves to be disciples of Reinach rather than Husserl. He was much closer in age and had excellent rapport with them.

It did not take her long to become an integral part of the Philosophical Circle. Georg Moskiewicz, who had been in Göttingen before and who had now returned for further study, simply took Edith Stein and her friend Rose Guttmann along to the next weekly meeting, and it was only later that the two newcomers discovered that their immediate acceptance into this select inner circle of Husserl students was not something they ought to have taken for granted. In Edith Stein's *Life in a Jewish Family,* her chapter on her years as a student in Göttingen offers telling glimpses of the various fellow-students and their different personalities, but they all apparently shared in an enthusiasm for the new field of phenomenology which Husserl had revealed to them and which they now explored and developed together. Eventually, the paths of teacher and pupils were to lead in different directions, but they remained friends and exchanged ideas, critiqued each other's work and published various Festschrifts together for years to come.

It would be remiss of me if I did not call attention to another very important influence at work on Edith Stein in Göttingen: Many of her teachers had been born Jewish and become Christian. For some, this may have been a purely pragmatic

115

step, designed to open up career possibilities in academia which would have been closed to them as Jews. Others, however, made the change as a result of their tendency to free themselves from all preconceived biases and unexamined ideas and strike out in new directions. Edith, a seeker after truth from way back, encountered in this new environment a liberating spirit that gave her permission, as it were, to embark on a new and independent path and look for new truths, unencumbered by the conditioning of home and family, which were now far away. Others had gone before her, they were pointing the way, and that helped to legitimize what she was now attempting on her own. Far be it from me to suggest that a woman of her intellect and independence of thought would embrace another religion merely because others were doing so. We have seen that Edith was not one to follow the advice or suggestions of friends or relatives, if she did not share their views. She would surely not do so now, unless her studies and search took her in a direction that led to another faith. The Husserls, the Reinachs, and Max Scheler all were converts to Christianity.

Edith Stein recalls how compellingly Scheler could speak about his faith during his lectures. Her confrontation with the religious fervor of Anna Reinach after the death of her young husband on the battlefield of World War I is often cited as one of the turning points in Edith Stein's spiritual development.

Although Edith wrote home regularly all her life, no letters by her hand have been preserved from that time, and it is doubtful that she would have shared the multitude of philosophical, intellectual and social impressions which overwhelmed her or the confusion she may have experienced over these challenges to pre-established thought patterns. Edith tended to keep her private thoughts private all her life. Generally speaking, what her letters communicated was only a small fraction of what moved her inwardly. Ultimately, whenever someone asked to know why she became a Catholic or why she chose Carmel as her destination, she would reply in Latin *Secretum meum mihi,*

(This secret belongs to me.) Years earlier, her family characterized Edith as a book with seven seals.[10] The mystery remained throughout her life.

With the outbreak of war in 1914, the mood and temper of the place changed. Edith had arrived in Göttingen in 1913, dreaming and hoping for an inspiring and instructive semester or two of intensive phenomenological study. She flourished under the guidance of capable instructors and the stimulating company of bright and eager fellow-students. Some she liked, for some she came to entertain romantic feelings, and some would maintain a lifelong friendship with her, with an exchange of letters over decades. But into the midst of this idyllic scenario burst the outbreak of the First World War. In 1914 it was, of course, referred to as "the World War", for no one could predict that a second, even more horrible and deadly, world war would follow only twenty-five years later. The young students were filled with patriotic zeal and nationalistic fervor. Most men and a few women rushed off to volunteer for service for the fatherland, Edith Stein among them. All at once their studies, books, exam schedules were forgotten, and war was the sole agenda. Göttingen and the university were in turmoil. Students left for their hometowns, professors reported for active duty.

And even though, later on, Edith was to return to Göttingen to resume her studies after she had served her term as Red Cross nurse in Mährisch-Weisskirchen, the magic had vanished from the town squares and the quaint restaurants of the college town. With the continued absence of the young men, the classrooms echoed with emptiness and worry over the men at the front consumed those who remained behind. Most of the changes Edith perceived upon her return to the university were not happy ones.

At the start of the war, Edith's cousin Richard had left for active service, while his young wife Nellie had closed their apartment, packed up the furniture and moved back to Breslau

117

into her father's house. Upon her return to Göttingen after her service as a field hospital nurse, Edith began to be aware that her cousin Richard and his wife Nellie were struggling with marital difficulties. In October 1915, while Richard was in a military hospital in Essen recovering from a war injury, Nellie visited him there and asked for a divorce. The Husserls already mourned their youngest son Wolfgang, dead in Flanders at seventeen. In 1915 Edith celebrated Christmas with the Philosophical Circle at the Reinachs. Husserl followed a call as a full professor to the University of Freiburg , where Edith eventually followed him to complete her doctorate and become his assistant. Göttingen was now a place of memory and nostalgia to which she returned for the burial of her beloved teacher Reinach, later to help organize his papers for eventual publication, and for some social occasions with friends still remaining in Göttingen.

CHAPTER 10

"Tante Edith"

Edith Stein had a warm relationship with her nephews and nieces. It almost appeared as if our intense affection was in inverse proportion to the amount of time she spent with us. She lived far from Breslau and her visits were rare but all the more eagerly anticipated and cherished. In an essay my brother Ernst Ludwig Biberstein wrote in 1983, fifty years after last seeing her, he says,

> She was something like the good fairy in one of those fairy tales which she would tell or read to us when she came to Breslau for a visit. While our other aunts, whom we saw daily and who frequently admonished us *in loco parentis* to tidiness, cleanliness and good behavior, we regarded as everyday occurrences, Tante Edith was part of a different world. Why was that? She was not the only one of her siblings who only appeared for a few weeks per year... For me it was first of all the fact that Tante Edith came from an area which I only knew from the field of saga and the romance of ballads and equated it with those. That's where she was "at home", in the geographic as well as allegorical sense. And as for the family in Breslau, she did not fit in there at all, despite all love and devotion which tied her to them. For somehow it always seemed to me that in that milieu there predominated an ashen, workaday mood which mistrusted all that life had to offer in the way of joyousness, light and pleasantness and deliberately turned its back to them. In the words of my father, one took the obligatory umbrage at everything . Now that was not at all true of "Tante Edith". She brought something festive along

on her visits, and in her presence, so it appeared, the everyday turned into a holiday mood. She radiated a cheerful serenity which communicated itself to us kids, and I had the impression that in her environs nothing brutal or painful could occur...

I still remember clearly how comfortable I felt in her presence and what limitless trust I had in her. She was the only relative of her generation who appeared to take us children seriously, who listened to us, and who spoke to us as her equal. We loved her almost to the point of infatuation...

This image of the beautiful fairy, however, dissolved after the revelation of her conversion and her impending entry into a monastery: Her resignation from the world which we had shared. For a boy of ten - and even for a sixty-year-old grandfather - that step was no longer compatible with the light and joyous being in whose proximity all anxieties and sorrows disappeared. That was to us a dark, nocturnal aspect which no one understood and which she neither could nor would explain to anyone.[1]

Already as a teenager, Edith proved her aptitude as a loving and patient caregiver to her sister Else's babies in Hamburg. In a reminiscence about her aunt, Ilse Gordon says:

...My mother often told me how that very young aunt took care of my brother, then only a few months old, as well as myself, aged about two, and how she was pretty reliable and skillful one time when my mother had to be away from the house for several hours...[2]

Ilse Gordon recalls an event which, she says, may seem trivial to others but which was important to her at the time.

When I was about fifteen and had outgrown my children's clothes and it was very difficult to buy new clothes, I received a navy blue wool skirt from Aunt Edith, used, but still in good condition...A few years later, when I was a university student and had very little money, she helped me again with a sum of money that today appears very small, but at the time sufficed to finance a two-week stay in a resort in the Lüneburger Heide.[3]

Much has been told about Edith's capable and devoted service as a Red Cross nurse during the First World War. Later, more informally, she had occasion to nurse her young nephews and nieces in times of illness. She was patient and gentle and beloved by her young charges. In her autobiographical book *Life in a Jewish Family* she relates how she took over the care of her two nephews, Wolfgang and Helmut, and her niece Lotte, her brother Arno's children, when all three came down with the flu at the same time and lay in bed with a high fever. In those days, long before antibiotics had been discovered and before even sulfa drugs existed, such childhood illnesses could last for weeks and were potentially fatal. For four-year-old Helmut, the illness culminated in pneumonia, and he was dangerously ill long after his siblings had recovered. An intimate companionship developed between the little patient and his aunt and continued long after he had recovered. Edith cheerfully entered into the small boy's world of make-believe and became his pretend-bride, and he dutifully shared cookies and candy with her.[4]

When asked about his memories about that incident, my cousin Wolf, Helmut's older brother, recalls in a letter of December 8, 1997:

> About 1920, I was 8, Helmut 4, Lotte 3, we were sick [with] pneumonia. Eva [another sister] was not [ill], she stayed with the aunts during that time. It took 4 weeks with me, but 3 months with Helmut; he was really very sick and Tante Edith nursed him.

Wolf also remembers how he and his cousins, Gerhard and Erika, participated in a playlet which their aunt Edith had written as entertainment for my parents' wedding celebration in December 1920. Gerhard played the stork, who was attempting to persuade two babies, one male and one female, to accompany him to the newlyweds, Hans and Erna Biberstein, to be their children. The amusing question-and-answer repartee entered into family legend. The text is preserved in our files, and I have translated it into English for interested readers. In 1987, my cousin Gerhard Stein, who was then 85 years old and who was the oldest of

Edith's nephews, recalled this event and some of the verses in this skit.

Of this cousin, Edith tells in her own words:

> ... How proud I was when, at the age of ten, I became an aunt for the first time! My mother also took her first grandson completely to her heart.[5]

Unfortunately there was a darker side to this love. My grandmother had a hard time developing a *modus vivendi* with her children's spouses. And Edith in her book *Life in a Jewish Family* generally supports her mother. She is critical of his mother Gertrude's[6] parenting skills and points out in none too gentle terms how this inexperienced mother neglected her child, reducing him to "a pitiable condition."

> When that happened, my mother took the little fellow into our home; and the solicitous care given him by his grandmother and aunts would soon undo all the damage. This procedure was to recur frequently. Every time my mother found the child sick and lacking proper care, she would wrap him in a big blanket, call a cab, and take him home with her. Gerhard was nursed through all his childhood ailments at our house. Naturally his *Grossmama* to whom, in any case, every child was attracted, was his all; she meant far more to him than his parents.[7]

Alas, she continues in this vein, expressing not only the trenchant criticism she and her mother had for Uncle Paul's wife, Trude, but also attributing to her inept childcare the death of Gerhard's younger brother Harald who succumbed to "a neglected case of scarlet fever" at the tender age of two. It is easy to see how this treatment given to his mother affected her son Gerhard when he read Edith's account in the 1960s. By then both his parents as well as his aunt Edith, who had told "tales out of school," so to speak, had been snuffed out in the Nazi Holocaust, and the pain of loss as well as the sadness at what Gerhard perceived as an unkind and far too critical assessment of his beloved mother overwhelmed him.

122

Each Friday night, that is Sabbath Eve, was celebrated in grandmother's house with a special dinner. My mother could not be there in time because of her millinery business. Therefore, after a while, only my father attended, and that remained that way even after Mother gave up her business. This absence of my mother at those Friday night dinners gave grandmother the opportunity to influence my father, with an adverse effect on his married life, until I was old enough to be able to put a stop to that.

Grandmother's distrust of my mother led to another unfortunate and very sad result. As a consequence of one night's attack of scarlet fever [?] my younger, two-year-old brother Harald got a streptococcus kidney infection. Since this was not recognized in time, Harald became very sick. Grandmother suggested to hire a nurse, who did not keep my brother Harald warm enough, and Harald died... Mother never got completely over losing this ...child. After that experience she always took care of me herself when I got sick, particularly since I was the only child she had left. She let nobody else nurse me. When I got scarlet fever and later even pneumonia, Mother pulled me through.

At a time when I had just entered third grade [Septima] in school, my parents sent me to grandmother for a few weeks, while their apartment was being renovated. The eighteen-year- old Edith took over the supervision of my homework...When the renovation was completed and my mother examined my schoolwork, she was shocked by my low grades. ... My teacher told mother that she was also surprised by my suddenly inadequate performance...The teacher emphasized also that a mother is the best supervisor of a child's homework. When Edith talked to the teacher afterwards, she must have got the same answer. After Mother took over, my grades became acceptable again pretty fast. This failure of her efforts must have been hard on Edith, who could not stand adverse results. [8]

Gerhard's stories go back further than those of any of her other nephews and nieces, because he was the oldest, only about ten years younger than this aunt. Here are a few anecdotes as remembered by Gerhard Stein:

When I was in elementary school, she was in the upper classes of Viktoriaschule, a girls' high school . Her achievements were so outstanding that she was given the Schiller prize in observance of [Friedrich] Schiller's 150th birthday [in 1907]. Grandma told me at the time how one day Edith came home, carrying a heavy load of books, Schiller's complete works.[9] At about the same time my parents' apartment was being renovated, so I was sent to Grandma's house and Edith took on the supervision of my

123

homework. That was not easy for her, due to my lack of ability, but she applied herself with great diligence.[10]

Not surprisingly, Gerhard Stein's perspective on some incidents differed from his aunt's. It confirms the old cliché that there are two sides to every story. Today, in hindsight, it pains us to read in Edith's book such a negative portrayal of her sister-in-law, with no appreciation of her musical talents and goodness of heart. Several months after my cousin Gerhard's death, I was given access to a series of letters sent to him by his parents in the years 1940 to 1942. These heartbreaking letters demonstrate the indomitable spirit of these two aging people, left behind in Breslau, Germany, hoping against hope that their quota number might be called in time to permit them to reach the American haven. Trying to find some diversion during those years of ever increasing duress, restrictive ordinances, insufficient food and fuel, they did more than just exist. Aunt Trude continued playing classical music in her home with like-minded friends. She played the viola in a chamber music ensemble. Sometimes there was a quartet, sometimes only a trio. As some of the participating musicians were deported, others took their places, until in July 1942, Paul and Trude's turn came, and they were taken to Theresienstadt, where both died a short time after their arrival. Their letters to their only son reflect great dignity, resignation and appreciation of the small pleasures they could still experience, through music and through receiving occasional food parcels which came via an acquaintance in Switzerland and through the help of the non-Jewish parents of Gerhard's wife Hertha.

Wolf, the eldest son of Arno Stein, recalls that Aunt Edith wrote poems for her mother's birthdays and had the grandchildren recite them for her. Being quite a few years younger, I only remember the skit Edith composed for Grandmother's 80th birthday, in 1929. By that time, my younger brother and I, aged seven and eight respectively, were already able to participate.. He and I were decked out in rococo costumes and powdered wigs, I in a stiff and awkward crinoline, my little brother in a black velvet jacket with white, frilled collar and cuffs, dancing a sedate minuet to Mozart's music. I envied the older cousins, for they were dressed as flappers and sang their songs to the tunes of the popular hits of the day, which, to me, seemed much more fun.

During our aunt's annual visits, we children especially looked forward to her story hours, when she would gather us around her and read us from some of her favorite tales, which were to become our favorites, too. My mother had established reading aloud to us as a favorite ritual at suppertime, since she and my father were accustomed to eating later, after we had been put to bed. But when our aunt came to visit, she held her own story hour, expanding the circle to include all available nieces and nephews. I remember especially the adventures of Nonny and Manny, two young boys in Iceland, who had the most exciting seafaring adventures. The author, Jan Svensson, was a consummate story teller, who spun his yarns with spellbinding excitement and suspense that kept all of us on the edge of our seats. When I discovered that my aunt knew the author personally, I asked her to help me write him a letter to let him know how much we had enjoyed his books. Some weeks later, I was thrilled to receive a reply from him, probably my first letter from a published author. If I remember correctly, he was by then a religious living in a monastery in his native Iceland.

This incident probably planted in me the first seeds of a longing to see the Scandinavian countries and of a romantic love for the ocean. The latter, I was able to satisfy for the first time when my mother traveled with us to the Baltic Sea, and we had our first encounter with the ocean. To satisfy my longing for Scandinavia, I had to wait until 1997, when my husband and I joined a tour of Denmark, Norway and Sweden. It was a brief tour, which offered us only a smattering of an acquaintance

125

with that landscape, and I still have not seen Iceland, where my heroes Nonny and Manny plied the rough waters of the North Sea.

My cousin Lotte Sachs, Wolf's youngest sister, writes:

> I...remember with pleasure us children sitting in a semicircle around her on the floor while she either told us stories or read to us; back in my mind they were stories about Iceland or Norway...[11]

Lotte, however, remembers also that "we were admonished to behave, to be quiet as she [Tante Edith] was writing (I guess an article or a book)." I also remember that we held her somehow in awe and respected her need for privacy and space. In that respect, she must have changed over earlier times, when she would allow her niece Erika to play quietly in her study.

> The child was greatly attached to me. She loved to be in my room while I was working. I would put her down on the carpet and give her a book that had many illustrations. Then she would be silent, keep busy, and never disturb me. ..Nor did she demand any other entertainment but remained quiet and contented until someone came to get her.[12]

My own memories are quite different. The door to Aunt Edith's study was typically shut, and we children were outside, while she was either writing or reading at her desk or entertaining one of her many visitors. At such times, we could hear the sounds of quiet and serious conversation. When our aunt was ready to spend some time with any of us, she would appear with a quiet smile and a welcoming word. Those occasions were prized by us, and we recall such precious moments even today.

I have no doubt that Aunt Edith, who had no children of her own, felt real affection for her nephews and nieces and took an interest in their lives. In her exchange of letters with me, she always responded with sympathetic interest to my concerns and worries. In the nineteen thirties, it was at times a painful daily struggle for me to attend school as the only Jewish student left in the entire school. I often felt that I had to abandon my real self when I left home and enter into the world in which Aryan ideology and anti-Semitic propaganda prevailed, where almost everyone but I belonged to the BDM (Bund deutscher Mädchen, i.e. Alliance of German Girls) and wore a brown uniform and a swastika pin. In school I had to guard every word and speak only what was politically correct or safe. At such times I would plead with my father to allow me to transfer to the Jewish high school, but he remained adamant: I had to stand my ground, maintain my right to study at the municipal school. I had to study hard and do my very best. No one should be able to find fault with my work on legitimate grounds. The burden was heavy, and Aunt Edith would occasionally write me an encouraging note, sensing my difficulties. Her letters would at times mention that it was too bad that I could not drop in to visit her in the cloistered serenity of her Carmelite home; I might find peace and healing there. It was not to be. Even when we left Germany in February 1939, we were unable to arrange a stop in Echt, Holland, where my aunt was living by then. In retrospect, the peace and tranquility she spoke about may seem illusory, seeing how she herself was later abruptly torn from the safety of these walls and taken to her death. And yet I am sure the peace she found within these halls was really within herself. Could she have shared this inner peace with her troubled relatives?

When my cousin Lotte emigrated to America, she stopped for a visit at the Carmel in Cologne. She was eighteen at the time, traveling alone and toward an uncertain future, leaving friends and relatives behind. Her mother had preceded her and paved the way for her. Her memory of this visit is brief and sketchy.

> I know I went by train overnight, arrived there early in the morning, took a cab to the convent. There I saw her through the grille, I guess we must have talked some; I ate breakfast. She handed me a little book which I don't have any more (61 years later), and I returned to the train by cab.

127

I don't know if I was the last family member who visited her, I've always surmised that I was.[13]

There is, however, a sequel to this account. A few days after writing me this letter, my cousin found the booklet which Aunt Edith had given her as a memento of her visit. It was neither a religious tract, nor a missionary text designed to influence Lotte to turn toward Christianity, but a novella by Bjørnssen.[14] That fascinated me, for my mother's bookcase contained a complete set of Bjørnssen's works, and as a teenager I read many of his stories. I guess he must have been a favorite of Aunt Edith as well. My aunt's choice of a farewell gift to her young niece also throws light on her disinclination to make any sort of missionary attempts toward members of her own family. Aunt Edith maintained her own right to profess her faith according to her conscience, but at the same time she would not presume to take unfair advantage of her loving relationship to practice missionary activity among her relatives.

This takes on special significance in the light of a remark in the booklet *Kölner Selig- und Heiligsprechungsprozess der Dienerin Gottes Sr. Teresia Benedicta a Cruce (Edith Stein),* Cologne, 1962, in which the following statement is found:

> She did not show disappointment when God denied her the profoundly desired last meeting with her sister Erna and her children whom she hoped to influence religiously at this opportunity.[15]

I want to cite here another anecdote from this pamphlet. It appears in a chapter entitled "Humility" and is designed to demonstrate this quality in Edith Stein.

> God permitted that she got to hear tactless remarks by her fellow-novices about her [Jewish] origins. Once she showed [her Carmelite Sisters] photographs of her young nephews and nieces. "My Lord, do they look Jewish!" one Sister presumed to exclaim.[16]

I have little doubt that the photos mentioned here were of my brother and myself. I would not characterize Edith's silence in the face of such tactlessness as "humility." I am sure she was deeply hurt and also saddened by the realization that anti-Semitism was present even within the confines of her new Carmelite home, but nothing she might have responded could have remedied that situation.

I was really never presumptuous enough to consider myself Aunt Edith's favorite niece and have no idea how that adjective at times creeps into the literature. I really believe each of us nephews and nieces (there were eleven in all) had a special bond with her. We all corresponded with her, and for all of us, Tante Edith had a special aura about her which distinguished her from all our other uncles and aunts. By "aura" I do not mean a halo of sainthood. To us, Aunt Edith was, is and remains, a beloved member of our family, whose warm human qualities will be a lasting legacy for us, irrespective of what may be happening to her public image or to her persona in the Church.

CHAPTER 11

My Mother, the Doctor

THE YOUNG WOMAN

It is a curious thing, but one never thinks of one's parents as young. They are quite simply our parents, and as such they are, to us, the older generation. Even when we were children and they young adults, I suppose they must have appeared to us as so much older that we could not visualize them as ever having been infants, children, young people growing up, playing, learning, flirting, falling in love. All that takes a leap of imagination which you cannot expect from the very young. Only when we had reached our late teens or early twenties did it occur to us to see our parents as individuals, as people.

Mother was the sixth of seven children, born in Lublinitz in Upper Silesia. Shortly after her birth, the family moved to Breslau. I have already mentioned the sudden death of my grandfather in 1893, when my mother was three years old and Grandmother's struggle to raise her large family and manage the lumber business at the same time. Times were hard at first, and money was scarce. Hence, only the "little ones", Erna and Edith, were privileged to attend the university, for, by the time they reached college age, their mother had achieved a measure of prosperity and the means to provide them with a university education.

Mother was always rather quiet and not very communicative; therefore the tales from her childhood were few. How poor they were in the early days is shown in the story of the apple. Grandmother gave little Erna a very large, red apple, with the instruction to hold onto it until her two older sisters Frieda and Rosa returned from school. Then the three of them were to share the fruit. The little girl stood wistfully waiting, holding the apple; but as time passed, her fingers began to poke, found a soft spot, pushed into the soggy flesh, succeeded in prying loose a piece of juicy apple and slipped it hastily into the greedy mouth. Mmmm! That tasted so good! No way could she be satisfied with such a tiny bite. Again the index finger poked and pried, and again it dislodged some apple. Well, by the time the girls came home from school, what little Erna held in her hand was merely the messy, scooped-out shell of a once crisp, round apple. Oh, shucks! That wasn't what she had intended. Still she was punished, because her greed had deprived Frieda and Rosa of their after-school snack.

When Erna was about four or five, she had a tremendous longing for a doll. For her birthday, she wanted only a doll. How she yearned for it, craved it, imagined it in every detail, this dream doll she had on her mind! She could hardly wait. The night before her birthday, she lay awake for hours with excitement. In fact during the wee hours of the morning, before the household awoke, she tiptoed to the living-room, where she suspected her family had set up a birthday table for her, and there in the dim light, the coveted doll sat waiting for her. Later, of course, when the big moment arrived and she was led into the room to view her birthday gifts, with all the family watching, she had to feign total surprise. I relished this story when I first heard it. It proved that our mother, too, had been a kid, nosy, sneaky, and not always perfect as children are supposed to believe their mothers to be.

131

Mother was a diligent, conscientious student, with a facility for languages and literature. What she had no talent for was art. Most particularly, she could not draw a straight line without a ruler. Her art teacher expected only mediocre work from her. Therefore, once, when Erna surprised herself and the teacher by contriving to draw a flawlessly straight line, the teacher unhesitatingly accused her of cheating by using a ruler. Erna, who was nothing if not scrupulously honest, pleaded innocence, but to no avail. The teacher carefully entered a black mark for cheating in her record book. Now Grandmother held all teachers in great respect and insisted that her children do likewise. If in doubt, she sided with the teacher. In this instance, however, she was outraged at the injustice done to her child. She could not take time off from her business, so she delegated her oldest daughter to visit the school and speak to the teacher. Else had to tell the art teacher in no uncertain terms that Erna never lied, that if she said she had drawn the line freehand, then she had surely done so. Whether the teacher ever deleted the reprimand from her record book, is not preserved in our archives nor in my mind, but the point was made; my mother's honor was restored.

After Grandmother bought the house on Michaelisstrasse, there was plenty of room, and with cousins, uncles. and aunts dropping in and out-of-town relatives coming for extended stays, the house was always full of life. Even decades later, Father would tease Mother with the name of Hans Horowitz, a cousin who had a great fondness for her. They hung around together, Erna and Hans, while Erna's younger sister Edith stuck with his twin brother Franz.

How uncle David, the pharmacist, persuaded Mother to study medicine has been mentioned earlier. She accepted his argument that she should choose a course of study that would not lead to a dead end but to a profession she could practice and with which she could make a living. One had to be realistic and acknowledge that the prospects for a Jew pursuing a career in academia were exceedingly limited, if not totally closed.

The demanding medical curriculum apparently did not deter my mother. She met all requirements, and when she took her *Staatsexamen* (state boards), she did very well. The outbreak of the war soon thereafter propelled her immediately into a busy residency which might not have been accessible to a woman in peace time; but since most of the young male doctors had been called up, there was urgent demand for the young women. Mother used to ride the ambulance or make house calls, day or night, to deliver babies or perform minor surgical procedures. In those days, a normal delivery was supervised by a midwife, and only when complications arose did the midwife summon a physician.

Erna and her friend Lilli Platau were serving their residency together. The chief of service may have had his prejudices about women doctors, but he could not get along without them now, and he had to admit, if grudgingly, that these two young women knew their stuff and were not afraid of long hours and hard work. Sometimes in later years, Mother would recount some scenes from those early years when an obstetrical practice was very different from what it is today.

Once she and Lilli responded to a call for medical assistance. A woman had gone into labor, but after hours of contractions, the baby still refused to be born. The two young women, carrying their instrument bags, climbed four flights of stairs to a walk-up apartment in a run-down building in a proletarian neighborhood. Conditions in the apartment were far from ideal. The woman in labor was not the wife of the man who had called them in but a former kitchen maid who was pregnant by him. The baby was in a breech position, and a spontaneous birth was out of the question. The wife was upset, but tried to help. The patient was exhausted and moaned with pain. The two young lady doctors took a quick survey of the situation. They would have to deliver by forceps, and while Erna would

133

perform this procedure, Lilli was to give the anesthetic which they had providentially brought along. The room was small and crowded, the bed in which the patient lay took up most of the space in it. To give the ether, Lilli would have to kneel on the bed, above the patient's head; but as she was about to climb on the bed to assume her position, she suddenly jumped, then whispered to her friend Erna, "There are bedbugs on this bed and I refuse to get on that mattress with the bedbugs!"

Erna was upset. The situation was desperate. The woman needed to be delivered of her struggling infant, fast. Lilli was adamant. Erna, determined, felt she had no choice but to go ahead, with or without anesthesia. She had all bystanders hold the unfortunate woman while she applied the forceps and delivered the baby. Fortunately, the patient proved to have tremendous stamina, and despite much yelling and screaming, after it was all over, mother and baby were in good shape. My mother never forgot this incident and how she had "sweated blood."

THE WIFE

Mother decided to open an office for obstetrics and gynecology on the street floor of her mother's house on Michaelisstrasse 38. The war was over, and my parents were married. They had married on Dec. 5, 1920 and they lived in Grandmother Stein's house. The downstairs office rooms were not elegant but certainly adequate, furnished with heavy oak furniture and without the sterile look of most medical offices. The neighborhood was not affluent, and Mother's patients were the wives of workers or lower civil service employees. Most of them were covered by health insurance, few were private patients. Mother was a quiet, kind, skilled doctor; she did not pamper or flatter her patients, but she was never rough or rude, and she soon won a large following. Father was on the staff of the University Hospital, on the faculty for Dermatology and Venereal Diseases, but had no private practice. He was on salary, while Mother had a private practice. Father had a fairly

134

regular schedule, but Mother had to be prepared for night calls and emergencies.

When my brother and I were of school age, we were used to coming home in the early afternoon and being greeted by Mother herself, wearing her white coat and looking very professional, but finding time for a quick kiss and a word of welcome. This was the time of her office hours. Later, after the last patient had left, she would emerge from her office, look for us and inquire about our school day. Sometimes she would go to my grandmother's kitchen and take a cup of coffee with her sister Rosa. She liked living in the same house with them; that way she could easily stop in to see her mother every day and be close to her family. We kids liked it too. If Mother was with a patient, we could always visit with Tante Rosa, who would be in the kitchen, baking something, and usually there would be a wooden spoon to lick clean, or a piece of flat noodle dough which she might toast for us on the hot surface of the cookstove and which tasted delicious. She would have these or other goodies for us to munch, and we would unpack the latest stories from school. Or she would tell us the news of her day, who had written, who was coming to visit, etc.

Mother always did the shopping in the morning, going to the butcher, or the fishmarket, the bakery and the grocery store. Vegetables were usually delivered; you could phone or take a shopping list to the little greengrocery and select everything or simply leave the selection to them, and later the owner would bring everything over. Sometimes we would go to the poultry lady and buy a chicken or pigeon, or a goose for the holiday. When we kids had no school, we would accompany Mother to the stores, and sometimes the lady in the butcher shop would hand us a slice of salami, or the bakery woman would offer us a cookie.

Trips to the department store were rarer. Mother was a busy woman, so she did not spend much time on shopping sprees. She prided herself on being a fast clothes shopper. She was fond of telling how one time she went downtown to buy herself a dress at a fashionable dress shop. While she was there, she got an emergency call at home, so the maid called the store immediately, and Mother was called to the phone.

"All right," Mother said, " Tell the patient I am coming right back. I'll be there in twenty minutes."

Anna, the maid, said, "Too bad, Frau Doktor, that you can't finish your shopping now."

"Oh, don't worry," replied my Mother, "I'm all finished with that, I was ready to leave anyhow."

She was the kind of woman that people confided in. Nephews and nieces, friends, sisters and brothers would pour out their troubles to her and find a patient ear and a sympathetic heart. She spoke little, but she let them know she was there for them when they needed her. Closest to her was her younger sister Edith. They were close in age, and as they grew up they had many interests in common. When Edith decided to study philosophy, her path began to diverge from that of her sister and other medical students, and she left Breslau to study in Göttingen.

Erna and Edith, however, remained very close, and when Edith decided to become a Catholic, she divulged her secret first to my mother, asking her to break the news to "Mama." It was a stunning blow to the entire family, and Mother knew how deeply it would grieve my grandmother. Yet she herself always professed an attitude of tolerant acceptance, even though she did not fully understand her sister, and throughout her life took care to show Edith her continued love and never once thought of rejecting her.

We called her "Muttel"[1], and though she was never demonstrative in her love for us, it was simply there, an even warmth, an enveloping affection that radiated from her to us. I believe she played no favorites, loving both Ernie and me equally. Since we were so close in age, most of the activities we were involved in included both of us. When she took us to the zoo, we both went, when she read us stories, we both listened.

Story time was usually in the evening. Father did not get home until eight or nine, so Ernie and I had our supper about seven, and Mother would read to us. First there were fairy tales by the Brothers Grimm or Hans Christian Andersen. Later she would choose books and read them to us, one or two chapters each evening. *Helen's Children* was an amusing tale of two mischievous children left in the care of their uncle, and his pathetic attempts to cope with them. Another favorite was *Dr. Doolittle*. Mother read us several books in that series relating the adventures of the droll little animal doctor and the animals he befriended. Before bedtime, Muttel would sometimes sing for us. She sang of the two grenadiers who came back from imprisonment in Russia or of Archibald Douglas, the faithful old servant who has fallen from grace with his beloved Scottish master. There were songs by Brahms and Schubert, Beethoven and Hugo Wolf, and most of them were sad and beautiful. She would accompany herself on the piano. It was a magic time in which her songs were for us alone, and we listened spellbound.

As we grew older, Mother would tell us the plot of an opera, then play some of the highlights and sing some of the famous arias. She wanted to familiarize us with these operas and planned to take us to an opera performance after we had gained some understanding of what we would see and hear. Among the operas she introduced us to were Weber's *Freischütz,* Mozart's *Zauberflöte*, Lortzing's *Zar und Zimmermann,* Humperdinck's *Hänsel and Gretel.* This last was the only opera we saw before 1933, at the Breslau Stadttheater, the local opera house. After National Socialism came to power in Germany and all the Jewish performers were fired, my parents boycotted the opera and theatre. They would only attend the performances of the *Jüdischer Kulturbund* (Jewish Cultural

137

Federation), and under its auspices we saw an unforgettable performance of the *Marriage of Figaro.*

After we left Germany, Muttel never sang again, and we had to leave our beautiful grand piano behind, so she did not play either. I wondered sometimes, as she grew old, whether she would have enjoyed resuming her music, or whether a piano would have merely reminded her painfully of the things she had lost and the people who were gone from her life forever. Mother was strong and tough. She went through very difficult years in New York trying to make a new life for herself and her family. She prepared for her medical exams, kept house, cooked and cleaned, corresponded with friends and relatives scattered all over the world, and tried to cheer and encourage Father, whose psyche was then in a very vulnerable, precarious state. She herself suffered depression at that time, much of it caused by the dreadful news from Germany and the worry over the four siblings who had remained in Nazi Europe. Yet somehow, my parents persevered and achieved their goal, obtaining their New York State medical licenses.

Mother was very unhappy with the negative attitudes she encountered as a foreigner and a woman in the American medical profession.. She managed to be admitted to the staff of a hospital in Brooklyn, so that she could attend to patients there, but without being a Diplomat of the Board of Gynecology and Obstetrics, she was not permitted to perform surgical procedures. If an obstetric patient required a Caesarian section, she would have to call in a colleague with the required specialist's rating.[2] It seemed to her the ultimate chicanery after a lifetime of experience in that specialty.

It suited my mother, in a way, that in 1944, when she was fifty-four years old, she became a grandmother. Times were precarious; the world was at war. My husband Alfred was slated for overseas assignment when our baby's birth was imminent. I, of course, had to leave my job. My parents very readily made room for us, me and the new baby, in their apartment. Not only that, but Mother with nonchalance, as though it was the most natural thing in the world, offered to take care of her first grandchild during the day while I worked at Cooper Union Library. Obviously, she could not pursue her medical career with an infant clinging to her apron strings. However, I feel sure that she would not have taken on the care of her grandson, unless she was resigned to giving up her chance of a meaningful medical practice. In fact, I sometimes think that this was a welcome alibi for her, since she had only reluctantly, and only at father's insistence, taken the laborious steps necessary to qualify for her medical license in this country. She was at best ambivalent about her goals and may have used her grandson Ronnie as a (welcome?) excuse. The final blow to her medical career came in 1950, when she reached her sixtieth birthday. She received a letter informing her that the hospital was terminating her staff privileges because she had reached the age limit.

From then on Mother's practice declined even further, although her shingle hung outside our apartment in Brooklyn and she shared Father's office in Manhattan. She felt rejected by the American medical establishment and she did not have the stomach to fight for her status any more.

Mother was to become extremely attached to her first grandchild for whom she cared full-time for a whole year and after that part-time until we moved out of town five years later. Ronnie loved his grandparents fiercely, and I occasionally felt twinges of jealousy when I realized how much more Ronnie shared with them than with me. For years his relationship with his grandparents Biberstein was very special because of the closeness with which his early life had been interwoven with theirs.

While Mother's practice declined during the nineteen fifties and sixties, Father's practice continued to be busy, and he went to his office every day and taught graduate courses in dermatology at NYU - Bellevue Medical Center.

139

Mother's personality stood in the shadow of his, which was much more flamboyant and colorful. Yet as he knew himself to be very ill with heart disease, he leaned increasingly upon her quiet strength. Not only was she always prepared to render emergency aid with an injection, she would pick him up at the office so he would not have to brave the cold winter winds alone, suffered anxiety in his behalf on those occasions, and let him take out his frustrations on her when he was unhappily confined in the hospital after an attack of edema. Their travels became a dubious pleasure, because sometimes his body did not tolerate the changes of climate or altitude well.

During the summer of 1965, our parents decided to vacation in Yosemite Valley and from there travel to Davis for the Bar Mitzvah of their grandson Michael. It turned out to be a bad time for Father. He suffered discomfort almost every day from shortness of breath and edema, had to have oxygen available in his hotel room, and only very seldom got out to walk slowly on level terrain near the hotel. Mother hovered over him anxiously, and we were prepared for the worst. By the time they left for Davis, his condition had improved, and Michael's Bar Mitzvah in early September was a great joy for him. In retrospect, this was literally the last family celebration he was to experience in his life, as he died in November of the same year.

THE MARRIAGE

Mother and Father were married for almost forty-five years. They fell in love as students, and because they lived in stressful and tumultuous times, they did not marry until they were twenty-nine and thirty years old respectively. Father had vowed that whoever took him for a husband would also have to accept into the household his mother who was severely ill with heart disease and to whom he owed all the devotion and care he was capable of. Yet in those difficult postwar years, there was no way that the young couple could find suitable accommodations for themselves and his mother. That would

140

have to wait. Meanwhile Hans and Erna would live in the attic apartment of Grandma Stein's house. While this was not an ideal arrangement, it gave them a roof over their heads as they started out in life together. And Grandma Biberstein could remain in her apartment on Augustastrasse in the south of Breslau. It was not what our Father had dreamed of, but until conditions got better and housing more plentiful, it would have to do. Nevertheless, in an unusually frank moment my mother once related to me how on her wedding night her husband had wept bitterly because he had not kept his promise to take his mother into his home when he married. He cried and cried, and his young wife did not quite know whether to burst into tears as well or to try to comfort him. It was perhaps an inauspicious beginning for a marriage which would survive many stresses and tensions but would grow firm and lasting and give both of them strength and happiness.

Father used to say, "No one can look inside a marriage."

I believe this is true. My aunt Edith in her autobiography had much to say about the torment that father caused my mother by his unreasonably demanding attitudes, by acting at times like a peevish, spoiled child, and by his difficulties in getting along with his mother-in-law. Yet, when my parents read these passages, both stressed emphatically that there had never been any danger to the stability of their marriage over these issues, never any doubt in their minds that they belonged together. It may appear contradictory that a woman who functioned independently and competently in her profession was at the same time yielding and conciliatory in her marriage relationship. These very qualities undoubtedly contributed to the peace and harmony which prevailed in her contacts with Father's mother, while she lived in our house. Grandma Biberstein moved into our house in 1928. Her relations with her maid Anna were stormy and occasionally punctuated by the maid's angry threats to leave and father's peacemaking efforts. They worked, for Anna remained years beyond my

141

grandmother's death in 1934 and was with us until we left Germany in February 1939. Grandma's moods and arbitrariness, her suspicions and complaints about imaginary insults were hard to take, but Mother remained calm and did not bear grudges. For this she was rewarded with Grandmother's half-hearted respect and, probably, as much affection as Grandmother was capable of giving her. Mother knew that much of Grandmother's peevishness could be attributed to her arteriosclerosis, and so she forgave her much. I can still see the two of them going out for a walk. Grandmother could only move very slowly. On one such day it was so bitter cold that I wondered how they could stand it out in the cold, moving at a snail's pace. My grandmother Dorothea Biberstein died in 1934 and was buried next to her own mother in the cemetery at Cosel[3] in Breslau. Father took her death very hard and from then on every Sunday he would take his family out to the cemetery to stand at her graveside for a few minutes. It was a long trolley ride to the cemetery and back, but it became a tradition which continued until he left for America in the summer of 1938.

When, in June 1995, we returned to the city of our birth for the first time since we had left, we drove out to the cemetery to look for my grandmother's grave. The cemetery was a tangle of weeds, almost impenetrable. We searched in this wilderness for over an hour, but could not locate the graves of my grandmother Dorothea or my great grandmother Ernestine. I thought of the care and expense my father had lavished on selecting the gravestone of green porphyry and the many trips we had made as a family to this spot before we had to leave. My grandmother's grave may be lost, the marker may have been stolen, but her memory is alive in my mind and heart, here in the New World, too.

THE WIDOW

We were really uncertain how Father's death would affect Muttel. They had been so close, especially in the last years, when they lived together, just the two of them. Their mutual dependence seemed very great, yet Muttel was self-sufficient, her character strong and solid. As it turned out, she coped remarkably well with her single life. Mother remained in her apartment for some eight years after his death. Mother went out to concerts and operas, visited and received friends. She traveled to Europe several times and once with us to Israel. She was a favorite guest because of her unpretentious, undemanding habits and gratitude for the smallest favors. Mother had a remarkable rapport with her grandchildren, visited Jon and Rose[4] in Colorado and later in Encino, CA and Ron and Nan[5] and their two children in Los Angeles. She maintained a far-flung correspondence with relatives and friends all over the world, and she kept in contact with the many institutions and individuals who were researching the life and work of her youngest sister, Edith Stein.

Mother was not dazzled by the prospect of sainthood for Edith. She saw her task in providing factual information wherever possible, and guarding against misrepresentation and distortion of facts in the transmittal of Edith's life story. Mother could not accept the concept of Edith's martyrdom, because, besides Edith, Mother had lost two other sisters and a brother to the Nazi machinery of destruction, to say nothing of the millions of others who also lost their lives in this Holocaust. Why speak of the martyrdom of Edith Stein, why single her out, when the identical fate was meted out again and again? Where was true meaning? What was the point? They were Jews. They were eliminated. And the world watched in silence, saying nothing, doing nothing. That is the horror of it, the totality of it.

Mother loved Edith, loved her perhaps more than her other sisters and brothers, because they were the closest in age, like twins, the children of their mother's later years, the children who grew up fatherless. She loved her because their minds were compatible, because she was bright and gifted and fun to be with, but her death, dear God! her death was no more bitter,

143

no more horrible, no more significant than the deaths of Rosa, or Frieda or Paul. And she used to tell us she would have infinitely preferred a living sister to a dead saint.

With her good health and alertness, Mother was the exception among her contemporaries. Most of her friends were ailing, and this depressed her. She would keep in touch with them, and in her regular telephone conversations with us report to us on one friend's hip replacement surgery and another one's stroke. Living in her own apartment, Mother became very concerned that something might happen to her, and no one would know. She asked several friends and neighbors to telephone her regularly to make sure that she was all right and she wanted at all times to know where her children could be reached, whether at home or on vacation.

She enjoyed getting out, visiting us, traveling to California and being in touch with her grandchildren. They did not write her often, but when she heard from them and received photographs, it lit up her day, her face. In her phone calls to us she would report all events, letters received, phone calls, visits, and all the good and bad news among her friends and acquaintances.

Our phone seldom rings now at 10:30 a.m. on Sunday. That used to be Muttel. You could set your watch by her call. It was so cozy talking to her on Sunday morning at breakfast. On Wednesday evenings we would call her. On Sundays, she would also hear from Ernie and Hannah in Davis. One of the biggest thrills she experienced was on October 26, 1976. That afternoon, when I returned from work, she called me on the phone to notify me of the arrival of our grandson Eric. It happened that he was born that morning, on a week day, and Jon could not reach us; we were both at work. So he called Grandma. What a joy for her to be the first to find out about the baby, her newest great-grandson.

144

Undemanding as she was, she would seldom come right out and ask for something she wanted. On the other hand, there were Sundays when she was staying with us and we would have irregular meals. We might eat a late and rather filling breakfast; then we might not think about eating for a long time. That was not for her. Come 1 p.m., her stomach let her know that it was lunchtime.

"Frankly," she would say, "I must admit, I could do with a bit to eat." She had a hearty appetite, always. All her life, Mother was extremely anxious not to bother, not to disturb, not to impose. One of her big worries in the last years of her life had been the possibility that she might become a burden to anyone. She was eager to remain self-sufficient, independent. She kept her own apartment, did her marketing every day. As she had lived, so she died. It happened during a visit to her son Ernie and his family in California. On the day before she died, she was stricken by a massive coronary attack. It happened to be Saturday morning, and together with her son and daughter-in-law, she was planning to go to San Francisco for a play, lunch with a friend, and dinner with her granddaughter Helen. When it became obvious that the outing to San Francisco would have to yield to an ambulance ride to the County Hospital, she demurred, "Here I go, spoiling your day for you."

Twenty-four hours later, she was dead.

On the day of the funeral, a blizzard struck New York, paralyzing traffic all over the city. Of the many friends and relatives who had planned to attend her funeral, only a handful braved the severe weather. It was a small, quiet funeral, for a very unassuming, modest woman. It was almost as if she had had a hand in arranging it that way, so as to spare her friends the inconvenience of having to come. I could not get that thought out of my mind that Friday. And the same thought recurred two days later, on Sunday. The snow was so deep that on Friday no vehicles could reach the cemetery, so that the

145

burial had to be postponed two days; even on Sunday we were told that the funeral chapel could send only one limousine. So when we got to Cedar Park Cemetery in New Jersey, the vast burial grounds were covered with a thick blanket of snow. A path the width of one car had been cleared. There were just five of us in the limousine, Bernie Cohn, the rabbi and my brother's brother-in-law, Ernie and Hannah, Alfred and I. A second car had brought two nieces of my father and their spouses. Because they lived nearby, they had ventured out, so that altogether we were about ten. We all crowded around the gravestone, looking down at the coffin which had already been lowered into the ground, and listened to a short prayer service, then dug into the frozen dirt pile to loosen a few clods of earth to cast down according to tradition.

Mercifully, a bright sun shone down and made the snow sparkle like diamonds. Mother was being buried right next to Father, in the very spot where she had always stood when visiting Father's grave. That was a poignant memory of her, alive here in this same spot, not so long before. She is gone now; we are now the older generation. One thing I know though. It doesn't all end there, with the burial. I am still saying good-bye to Muttel. She is here, with us, often! The Lord has given, the Lord has taken. That is how the ancient formula goes. But the way I see it, what the Lord has given, the Lord can never completely take away. Therefore, let the name of the Lord be blessed.

CHAPTER 12

Those who Perished

Edith Stein is often called a "martyr of the Holocaust". At the same time, we don't very often see the name of her sister Rosa mentioned, even though she shared her fate and died, so far as we know, together with her, on the same day, in the same way. There are two other siblings of Edith, as well as other relatives, who were victims of the Holocaust. In the absence of graves or headstones to mark the places where their remains may be buried, it is incumbent upon us, their survivors, to recall them one by one, with affection, and to make sure their memory is not lost. Sadly, not enough is known about the way and the date of their deaths in each case, but we can piece together the history of their lives and their deaths insofar as possible.

Paul Stein (1872-1943) was the oldest in the family, a handsome young man in the familiar family photo taken a few years after Father Siegfried had died. Paul was twenty-one at the time of his father's sudden death in August 1893, and Edith was not quite two. She lovingly recalls how Paul would carry her on his shoulders and regale her with stories from German literature at an age when she could hardly be expected to absorb such lore. Yet like a sponge, her brain took in much of what he recited, and Paul delighted in her bright precocity. Paul was a young man of great promise and intellectual curiosity, but as a child he had had scarlet fever and Grandmother believed that it had affected his personality in some way.

> [There was, in 1880,] an epidemic of scarlet fever in Gleiwitz. (Such epidemics occurred frequently in Upper Silesia.) During this particular one, little Hedwig, a particularly lovable child who had already begun to be a help to her mother, succumbed to the fever. My eldest brother Paul recovered, but my mother thinks the illness changed him. He had been a very handsome, highly-talented, lively child. Afterwards he became a quiet, shy, retiring person who was never able to make the most of himself or of his gifts.[1]

He became what educators today would term "an underachiever" all his life. Money was tight, and so he did not get a university education. Edith tells us that "perhaps a way would have been found after all, had he insisted upon it. But he was not one to assert himself."[2] Because of his passion for reading, he began an apprenticeship in a bookstore, but did not last in this job. He then tried bookkeeping in his mother's business, but later turned this job over to his younger brother and became an apprentice in a banking firm. Although it must have been less than congenial work for him, he worked conscientiously in the bank, in a clerical position for decades, without getting the recognition due him. His spare time was devoted to his hobbies, books, music and hiking. His son Gerhard relates:

> As good friends, my father and I spent Sunday afternoon regularly ...hiking on trails near our hometown of Breslau. At another time we covered nearly 50 miles [sic!] on the mountain range of the *Riesengebirge* on a one-day hike. Again at another time Father and I climbed the *Wildspitze*, a peak in the *Ötztaler Alps and Austria's second highest mountain, from the Braunschweiger Hut* in a twelve-hour glacier tour. It was perhaps the most beautiful day and the best long-distance panoramic view from the peak in my entire mountaineering experience.[3]

He retired prematurely and, Edith remarks in her book, that he was probably happier in his retirement than ever before in his life, devoting himself to his interests and living a leisurely, though economically restricted existence on the small pension he had earned. In an essay my brother wrote in October 1995, he recalls with affectionate humor this uncle, with whom he had great rapport:

> He was a rather quiet sort, only rarely entering the women's chitchat...until something was mentioned touching on books, plays, or music. Then he could become animated, articulate, eloquent, and even demonstrative. He would get up and act out scenes from operas with most graphic and sometimes terrifying persuasiveness. Most vivid in my mind is his depiction...of the witch from Humperdinck's *Hänsel and Gretel*. Assuming a posture of horrible deformity and contorting his face into a frightening grimace, he would grab some nearby implement for a crutch —a poker, a broom, or an umbrella — and hobble around while screeching out the lyrics, punctuated by devilish laughter.

> ...He never spoke down to us, never seemed to want to improve our minds or manners, or push us into some imagined right direction as most of the other relatives of his generation were incessantly doing. Without ulterior agenda, he was simply enjoying the company and the conversation with an equal partner. Though quite sociable and communicative, when given the opportunity, he seemed contented by himself, self-contained and self-sufficient...

> Poor Uncle Paul! Properly, he should have been allowed to live out his modest Rockwellian idyll for which he was so admirably equipped. But [instead] both he and Aunt Gertrude, past seventy by then, were taken from their cluttered home to disappear in one of Hitler's warehouses of death. Is there a chance, the visions of beauty that seemed to fill his inner life remained faithful to him to the end in those dreadful places? That might be a big order, even for Uncle Paul.[4]

His wife Gertrude, née Werther, whom he married over the objection of his mother by secretly eloping with her, was a musician, who also worked as a milliner. Actually, she was a milliner first, because, as one of seventeen siblings, she needed to earn a living; only later, when in her forties, she studied music. She taught and lectured; she played piano, violin and viola. My brother and I studied violin and piano with her for several dismal years; dismal, because I probably can't imagine two less promising music students than we were. Once a week, we would reluctantly wend our way towards their house on Yorkstrasse, where they lived in a cluttered apartment with a flock of canaries which my aunt raised, lavishing a great deal of time and affection on them. Since neither of us practiced our instruments, we made little progress and had little taste for the whole enterprise, and our poor aunt got few rewards for her efforts. She probably felt that she had to persevere, so as not to disappoint our parents, and our parents were loath to stop the lessons, so as not to offend Tante Trude, and so the sad charade continued. Our weekly trips to their house, however, gave us an opportunity to get to know them a lot better than might otherwise have been the case. Uncle Paul's remarks ranged far and wide, over literature, music, theatre, opera, crossword puzzles, jokes and, very carefully, politics. This was not entirely safe, as my uncle and aunt had a boarder, an elderly woman who lived with them and was not Jewish. Although she was often present during our visits, she was quite deaf, and it was not certain that "Muttel Noffke" could hear some of the irreverent comments concerning the Nazi regime which Uncle Paul allowed himself to mumble under his breath.

Paul and Trude had two sons, Gerhard and Harald. Harald died of scarlet fever at the age of two, while Gerhard grew to adulthood, became an electrical engineer, married a non-Jewish wife with whom he emigrated to the United States in the early nineteen -thirties, and fathered two daughters and one son. Gerhard lived to age eighty-six and, in the last year of his life, attended his aunt Edith's beatification in Cologne, together with two of his children and two granddaughters. Gerhard followed his wife into the Protestant religion, but retained a certain nostalgic loyalty to his Jewish roots. He remembered some prayers, in Hebrew, which he had learned to recite as a young boy, and after he died, his children found a copy of the *Sh'ma*[5], in Hebrew and English, in the drawer of his bedside table. Some time after his death, we came into possession of a series of letters and postcards written by his parents, Paul and Trude Stein, during the last years of their existence in Breslau, before deportation to the East. The letters cover a time period of November 28, 1939 to July 17, 1942. This last message, on a postcard addressed to Dr. Goldstein, an intermediary in Switzerland, tersely says:

> [Permit me to inform] you herewith [that] I, with my [wife], will leave Breslau and move to Theresienstadt in the Protectorate. Asking you to transmit this information to our children when the opportunity presents itself, I want to repeat my cordial thanks for all your effort up to now.
>
> Sincerely yours,
> Paul Stein.[6]

Nourished by the slim hope that one day, the quota number assigned to their "case" would be called up and they would be issued the all-important visa to enter the promised land, America, and join their son and his family, their beloved grandchildren, they valiantly maintained a life of dignity and courage in the face of ever greater economic deprivation.

> ..... in the meantime I received a waiting number 082095/082096... Mother and I know exactly that we both signed the three English application forms. I believe I may assume that on the basis of our quota number we have prospects of leaving the country in about five years, while, in your view, after your citizenship has been granted, we could join you in 3 years. ... I was told that a father, sent for by his son in the U.S.A., who had already received his citizenship, had been summoned by the Berlin Consulate for the purpose of having a preferential visa issued to him, and, despite having passed the exam, or the medical examination respectively, had to return without success.[7]

Note the hint of sarcasm in his reflections on the dim prospects for emigraton.

And yet, somehow, life continued and even provided some small pleasures and entertainment:

> Every Saturday we have "family day" here. Tante Clara, Tante Frieda and Eva come to us, and letters from all over the world are read. Formerly we drank freshly ground coffee

151

together. Since we no longer have any, we drink Russian tea of which I still have some. The letter from U.S.A. came [last Saturday] just after they had left, otherwise it would have been read aloud. We have been told that there is a new regulation in America, namely: Children can send for their parents, without being U.S. citizens, provided they have a monthly income of more than $160.00.

You'll be able to find out about that more easily. We hope that we'll be able to come to you in the not too distant future.[8]

Trude held weekly musicales in her home, at which she played the viola, inviting various amateur musicians to make up a trio or quartet.

Tomorrow our string quartet will play here (Schubert: *Death and the Maiden*). 2-9-41[9]

At our house, we now play music only in the afternoon, because the time permitted for going out in the evening is restricted. Mother plays the violin with an accompanist, or she plays the viola in a trio. Unfortunately, string quartets are inactive now, partly because of emigrations, partly because of disagreements among the participants.[10]

As various friends were deported, others took their place, so that the music never stopped, as long as my uncle and aunt remained in Breslau. With America's entry into the war in December 1941, letters could no longer be exchanged between Germany and America. Henceforth they stayed in contact with their son Gerhard via a Dr. Goldstein, a Swiss intermediary, who also was able to send them occasional food parcels, for which they would thank him profusely, for the delicious sardines, ten pieces per can, and the tasty canned tomato juice "of excellent quality, very useful for soups or as a fine sandwich spread".

Paul Stein and his wife Gertrude, were among 1,100 Jews from Breslau who, on July 27, 1942, were deported to Theresienstadt. According to data at Yad Vashem, they were on transport #1099, arriving in Theresienstadt July 27, 1942 . Uncle Paul died April 29, 1943, his wife on March 18. We visited Theresienstadt on July 3, 1995, 53 years after they got

152

there, and tried to imagine what their days in this so-called "model camp" would have been like. In a letter to Sr. Josephine Koeppel dated October 28, 1984, Gerhard Stein reflects with sadness, regret and a trace of guilt on the death of his parents: "Both died in the Nazi concentration camp at Theresienstadt (Terezin) in 1943 because of neglect and because of my ignorance and my lack of skill [in managing] to bring them to this country when there was still time to do this."

RED ROSES

Luxuriant roses
Planted in rows upon rows,
Here in the graveyard
Of Terezin.
A few markers with names
Some mass graves
Of unknown strangers
Brought here to die
Of typhus or malnutrition.
A large cross towers
Over one field of death,
A Jewish star rises
Over the other.
We stand and silently
Form with our lips
Words of *Kaddish*,[11]
But one thing troubles me:
Is it not *Hillul Hashem*[12]
To speak such words
In a place such as this?

Elfriede Tworoger (1881-1942) was "Tante Frieda" to us. She was short and chubby, and she lived in Grandmother's house with her daughter Erika. Frieda had been briefly married, but

153

her marriage had ended within a year or so, and she moved back to the parental home with a six-month-old baby girl.

Somehow it never seemed obvious to me that Tante Frieda was Erika's mother, for Erika was reared by a conglomerate of women, Grandmother, Aunt Frieda and Aunt Rosa together. I suppose my parents and Uncle Arno and his wife, Aunt Martha, contributed as well, since they all lived under the same roof. As an adult, Erika towered over her mother and appeared to treat her more like a pal than like someone to whom she owed respect and deference; there was undoubtedly warm affection between them. When my aunt Frieda's 25th wedding anniversary rolled around (an anniversary of a marriage that had lasted but the twinkling of an eye, my grandmother, in a moment of levity and dubious attempt at humor, placed upon her head a silver wreath to mark the occasion. Tante Frieda was somewhat annoyed and quickly yanked the ornament off her head, while the rest of us who witnessed the incident, stood by in silent embarrassment. Grandmother initially chuckled, but withdrew a bit shamefacedly as she discovered the inappropriateness of her "joke".

I have never heard my aunt speak of that disastrous marriage. She was older than Rosa by two years, and they were treated like twins, even though they were very different. Frieda tended to be docile and a bit phlegmatic, whereas Rosa was a wild kid, given to outbursts of rage. Hence she was nicknamed the lion. Edith tells us "Of all the children, she was the most difficult to raise." But even though Frieda had a hard time in school, she applied herself and enjoyed memorizing and reciting long ballads by Schiller and Uhland. She completed the *Höhere Mädchenschule* (Girls' High School) and subsequently took training in homemaking and bookkeeping. This training was to stand her in good stead throughout life, and she became a competent bookkeeper in her mother's business, the lumberyard, sharing with her mother and her brother Arno the small shed that served as an office. She also tended the vegetable garden and strawberry patch on that property. She enjoyed reading and often told us about the books she read, Gustav Freytag's *Soll und Haben*, Pauline Wengerov's autobiography, *Memoirs of a Grandmother*, letters of the Mendelssohn Family, and so on.

She was in charge of the sewing and mending for the whole family and she took pride and satisfaction in a tidy linen closet filled with fragrant, white, smoothly ironed and starched linen.

In an essay, my brother Ernst Ludwig Biberstein, describes her as follows:

> Tante Frieda, the wallflower in the family, who was constantly being bullied by her Mother, who was also her employer, and later to a certain extent also by her daughter, was a subdued being of limitless kindheartedness, but also with a definite sense of humor.[13]

Tante Frieda also knitted and crocheted. At the time, I had no enthusiasm for any kind of needlework, perhaps for the very reason that I was surrounded by so many relatives who excelled at this activity, but as an adult, as I took up knitting and crocheting as well as embroidery, I realized the origins of my interest and have always found such activity to be "my tranquilizer".

The difference in temperament between my aunts Frieda and Rosa jumps out at the reader of their letters. Rosa's letters frequently reflect discontent and weariness at the burden of work which she was expected to do.

In a letter dated Sept. 19, 1923, at age 39, she writes to Edith,

> This place is a kind of madhouse right now, we are at the end of our strength... Somehow we have to cope with the whole household, and that's awfully hard. There are mountains of mending, clothes which are in terrible condition, who can manage it all? And the children [of Arno and Martha] are hard to control, because there is no time. They are not used to obeying nor to doing their homework diligently. I feel terrible, physically and mentally beat, and, because of the many burdens I am irritable and hard to live with, and afterwards I want to take back everything I said and did.

155

Frieda, on the other hand, can find a reason for joy even in the drudgery of forced labor under almost desperate circumstances:

On a postcard addressed to her sister Rosa, who was then living in the Carmelite Monastery in Echt, Frieda, now forcibly "resettled" in Riebnig, in the Protectorate (formerly Czechoslovakia) and sharing a room with several women, writes:

> This week I had a lot of work; first I washed our laundry, then that of the entire community; it was a lot. Few laundresses. Boy, did I have sore muscles! But today, while ironing, I was happy about the whiteness. Our laundry supervisor is very capable, diligent, helping everyone. Once we can dry the laundry outdoors, it will be easier and better. -Our cultural entertainment is provided for us...Yesterday we had English lessons again...Tonight is a literary program.[14]

From Rybnik, Frieda and her fellow-Jews were sent to Theresienstadt, where she died some time later that same year. She was not quite sixty-one years of age. I do not know the cause of her death, but she came from a long-lived clan, and the two postcards from her pen show a steady, firm hand. I would guess that my aunt Frieda might have enjoyed many more years of productive life had she been permitted to live them out peacefully and normally.

TEREZIN—THE MODEL CAMP
A VISIT, JUNE 1995
HALL OF ARCHIVES—NO ADMITTANCE

We've come on a journey
To find, perhaps,
Traces of dear ones,
Whose last stop
Was Terezin.
Clutching a list of names,
We venture forth
Into the Hall of Archives.

156

Two ladies ably preside.
File drawers slide open,
Lists, endless lists,
Arrivals, departures,
Coming, from where?
Going to—who knows?
Dates have been noted
With utmost care.
The women's voices are gentle,
Compassionate.
They know that here,
Though decades have passed
The scabs reopen,
Blood may flow once more,
And tears, for sure.
Not all who were here,
Who passed through
Have papers to prove it.
The women console,
"Your grandmother—
Arrived on July 27
And she died, here's the date,
September 10,
Less than 2 months later.
Understand, she died here,
Not deported to Auschwitz.
Peacefully. Here."
Some who lived here,
Some who died here,
Or simply passed through,
Have their monument
In a file cabinet,
On a piece of paper,
And in our aching hearts.

Rosa Adelheid Stein (1883-1942), was given her maternal grandmother's name as a middle name, one of four girls born in the family that year who were named after her.

Rosa was almost ten when her father died. Rosa never married, whether for lack of desire or opportunity, I cannot say. It was never discussed in the family. I believe she was a mediocre student. She certainly did not receive a higher education. As an adult, however, she took courses in the Volkshochschule in Breslau, an academy for adult education

By the time I was born, "Tante Rosa" was in her late thirties. We children always felt especially close to her, because we had daily contact with her during our childhood. We lived in the same house. When we came home from school, our first stop often was the large kitchen, where Aunt Rosa was busy cooking or baking and would usually have some tasty tidbit for us.

My brother and I were the youngest of Auguste's grandchildren, and as such were probably somewhat spoiled. My recollections of Rosa appear to be much more positive than those of my older cousin, Lotte Sachs, who recalls her as having been very critical. I can believe this, because Rosa had strict notions of right and wrong and did not hesitate to express her views of other family members. She as well as Frieda and Grandmother, spurned all finery and luxury and lived very simply. Rosa was a fine cook and baker, and for all birthdays, she would bake the traditional Streuselkuchen (crumb cake). For the Sabbath, she baked the traditional braided loaves for their household and for ours as well.

In those years, the late twenties and early thirties, Germany was in a severe depression, with great poverty and large-scale unemployment. Door-to-door begging was a daily occurrence, and my aunt never let anyone go away empty-handed. However, she always gave the beggars food, never money, so that they would not spend it on drink. She would fix them a sandwich or a bowl of soup. Some of the beggars did not appreciate such a donation in kind, and occasionally a bowl of soup would be spitefully spilled on the steps leading to her front door. This would fill Aunt Rosa with indignation over the affront, the resulting mess, and the lack of appreciation of a kindness.

Another vivid memory I have has to do with Tante Rosa's care for an unfortunate child. A classmate of mine who was somewhat retarded — in retrospect I believe she may have suffered from Down's Syndrome - always came to school with welts all over her body. She was painfully thin. Our teachers would punish her because she could not sit still, wandered up and down in the classroom and paid little attention to directions. For these infractions of discipline, she was quite often caned. I did not understand what was wrong with her, but once I heard my parents talk about this child. Apparently she received little love and attention at home; she was what today we would call a "battered child." Once I found out, quite by chance, that Aunt Rosa was helping my little classmate with her homework, taking her home and giving her a bit of attention. I was only six years old, but I remember being surprised and proud that my aunt was involved in such work. It was the first time I had seen anyone treat this girl with affection. It changed my own attitude toward her, and I began to pay some attention to her myself. I gave her a shiny red hair ribbon once, but I am not sure whether that idea sprang from my own brain or whether it was my mother's suggestion. [The little girl's story had a tragic ending. She jumped into the Oder River, taking her own life when she was eight years old. My father could not get over it. He kept talking about this child, who, at such a young age had experienced such horror and cruelty that she could not see a way out.]

Another example of Rosa's caring for others was the fact that she visited a prisoner on death row in the penitentiary. I was older by then, and she mentioned to me that she was going to the prison to see him. All I remember was that his name was Martin Schmidt and that he had murdered someone. I was amazed that my aunt would go to visit such a person, but she explained briefly that even murderers need to know that they are not abandoned.

As I mentioned before, Rosa was the housekeeper in the household of her mother, which also included Rosa's older sister Frieda and Frieda's daughter Erika. My cousin Erika would tease her aunt by calling her "Drosselbart," after King Thrushbeard of one of Grimm's fairy tales. We would laugh, but I don't think Tante Rosa thought it was funny and did not appreciate having fun poked at her for her somewhat longish chin. Rosa had little of the humor that almost everyone else in the family possessed. She took life very seriously and, in doing so, contributed a certain dark mood, a negativism that communicated itself to her environment to an unfortunate degree.

In his character sketch of, and tribute to, our aunt Rosa, my brother states:

> For her, there were only duties, a constant "thou shalt" or, more often "thou shalt not". It appears likely to explain her dismal attitude toward life by pointing to her unsatisfying development and her subordinate position in the family... In retrospect, however, it is enough for me to state that Tante Rosa, during the years I knew her, was not a happy person and that, in my judgment, a number of reasons for this fact existed. She was, contrary to her inclination, the Cinderella who slaved away in the house, while her siblings, although not exactly dancing at the ball, yet practiced more or less respected professions in the world outside or had families of their own.[15]

Erika was a studious girl, aiming to be a teacher. She became a very observant Jew and later took courses at the Jewish Theological Seminary in Breslau; she frequently found herself at odds with her aunt Rosa over the observance of the Jewish dietary laws. Although their kitchen had always been kosher, my cousin now demanded a stricter adherence to these dietary rules and often criticized her aunt for not abiding by the letter of the law. Rosa, by then well on the way toward conversion to Catholicism, had a hard time taking all this seriously and resented her niece's criticism. Rosa delayed her baptism until after the death of her mother, out of respect and consideration and to spare her mother additional grief. I believe, however, that even before her formal conversion, she secretly followed Catholic ritual, used a rosary and attended mass. She was discreet about it, again out of consideration.

I never found out how it came about that Rosa followed her younger sister into Catholicism. We were at that time too young for such discussions, and my aunts, both Rosa and Edith, were conscientiously avoiding any conversation with us children that could have been interpreted as proselytizing. My father was extremely intent, and said so, that my aunts make no attempts at converting his children. He need not have worried; they sedulously avoided any semblance of such activity.

When we left for the United States in February of 1939, Frieda had a quota number for America, but it would mean a long wait. Rosa was in correspondence with a woman in Belgium, who was about to found a monastery for Tertiary Carmelites and was looking for a housekeeper.

> There are prospects of Rosa's getting into Belgium, to a Tertiary of our order.[16]

I believe this contact had been made via Edith, who was by then already in Holland. Rosa was looking forward to going, because the restrictions of life in Nazi Germany were becoming increasingly oppressive, and ever since the pogrom of November 9, 1938, very frightening. After that first experience of widespread violence against us Jews, we would say, "Anything is possible now." Rosa Stein had planned to take with her to Belgium most of the furniture and household linens from the combined household of the Steins. Since the lady who was to give her a home and a job in Belgium was setting up a new Carmelite establishment, she welcomed someone who also had the necessary household furnishings. At that time it was still possible for Jewish refugees emigrating from Germany to take their possessions with them, subject to certain restrictions.

Unfortunately, the entire project was a disaster, the woman a swindler, who had lured my aunt to Belgium under false pretenses in order to gain possession of Rosa's belongings and exploit her as an employee, expecting her to work long hours every day in a filthy, neglected environment. Rosa was desperately unhappy and somehow got word to her younger sister Edith, Sr. Teresia Benedicta a Cruce in Echt, Holland, asking her to please rescue her from this witch who had taken her in by lies and deceit.

We have a report by a certain woman by the name of Barbara[17], who was dispatched to the village where Rosa Stein had gone to work, somewhere between Maastricht and Lüttich. It was a difficult assignment, going to a strange place and looking into a situation in which a woman, who claimed to be founding a new Tertiary Order of Carmel, was keeping a refugee from the Nazis in virtual slavery. Upon arrival in the village, the messenger ascertained from the local priest, that the "old woman" had a bad reputation and the people of the village were looking for a pretext to get rid of her. But so far, she had been paying her rent punctually, giving the town no excuse for evicting her. The emissary from Echt finally managed to spirit Rosa Stein away after convincing her boss that she was unsuited to staying with her. Rosa was not permitted to take with her any of her belongings except what could fit into a small suitcase and, after some skillful persuasion, her "rescuer" managed to talk her oppressor out of another suitcase full of objects which had little value for her but were of sentimental value for Rosa. All the furniture, china and linens had to be left behind. Rosa Stein was just grateful to be free once more and looked forward to being reunited with her sister Edith.

I cannot say how long Rosa remained in her Belgian slavery; it could not have been more than a few months. A letter from Edith to my mother Erna Biberstein states that Rosa arrived from Belgium on July 1, 1939.

Even in Echt, things did not go smoothly for Rosa Stein. In a letter to Mother Petra Brüning, dated April 26, 1940, Edith reports that

> We had hoped that since she has at last been given a residence permit [in Holland] she could soon become an extern Sister. But our superiors (our dear Rev. Mother and the Father Provincial) think the time is not suitable for making such a change... They suggested Rosa become a Third Order member for the time being and that she wear the habit. It is a very painful disappointment for Rosa. She does not like the busy activity connected with being a portress, would much rather live inside the cloister...[18]

More disappointments for Rosa Stein! And yet we learn that she carried out her duties as portress in the Carmelite monastery of Echt faithfully and that she won friends in the town. When both sisters were arrested by the Gestapo, people from the town gathered around and showed their support, especially for Rosa, whom they knew because of her liaison with the outside world.

After all these years, it is still extremely painful for me to think about the tragic end of Rosa and Edith Stein, but I have wondered whether in those days and hours of horror and fear their togetherness may have given them strength and comfort. There is a passage in Jewish liturgy, concerning the slaughter of the martyrs. It says: "Beloved and true were they in life, and even in death they were not divided." That is how I picture Rosa and Edith. Alone, Edith could have found asylum in Switzerland, but she refused to accept refuge without Rosa, and in the end they met death together.

WILDFLOWER BOUQUET

Birkenau! Meadow of birches.
   Rural idyll, peaceful, pastoral
Here's a bouquet,
   Plucked from the field,
From earth newly fertile
With ashes, blood, excreta
   Of thousands of victims
Brought here to die.

Birkenau! I would have thought
   That for millenia
No life would sprout,
   No green grass grow
In your valley of thousandfold death,
   Where for a few incomprehensible
      years,
Madmen held sway, poison gas,
   Screams and beatings and pain.

The sighs of the dying
   Are heard no more.
And in the shallow ditch
   Next to the street where once
Goose-stepping boots struck the ground,
   Killer dogs barked,
Prisoners, skeleton-thin,
   Were herded to the showers
Whence no one returned,
   Now bloom golden buttercups
And bluebells.

   Grasses sway
In the light summer breeze,
   Gossamer cobwebs are spun
Between tall grasses, pearly with dew.

Dragon-flies zig-zag.
The day is quite lovely,
And my futile, belated tears
Water the buttercups,
The grasses of Birkenau.

Eva Stein (1915-1943) was the only one of my cousins who fell victim to the Holocaust. Eva was the second of my uncle Arno's and his wife Martha's four children. She was apparently retarded from birth. A psychiatrist who examined her in the thirties, diagnosed her to have a mental age of eight and stated that she would never go beyond that. Eva was a kind, innocent girl who wanted very much to be like the rest of us. She went to a regular elementary school and struggled hard to keep up. In her teen years, she learned to cook and bake and was proud of her skill in baking hallah, the braided bread that Jewish families eat on Shabbat. She was fairly athletic and could do the "circle on the beam" (*Bauchwelle*) expertly, for which I greatly admired her, since I could never equal that feat. She was tall and quite strong, affectionate and deeply attached to all the family. When we traveled, we always sent her postcards or letters, which she greatly appreciated. In her nuclear family, she was never given special treatment, nor did her parents attempt to get her special schooling or tutoring. They were great believers in "mainstreaming," a term which was not used in those days. Whether this was correct or not, I do not wish to say. My parents would criticize Uncle Arno and Aunt Martha for treating Eva as a normal youngster and, later on, for not making their other children aware that they might have to assume responsibility for Eva's support in later life. My aunt Martha gloried in her motherhood but had little patience for nursing her children through illnesses or coping with a "special child". It was probably Aunt Rosa who was most devoted to helping her with her homework and giving her some extra attention.

165

Martha Stein was in the fortunate position of being an American citizen. Although she had been born in Dresden, Germany, both her parents had American citizenship, and so she, too, was an American citizen. As such, she was able to emigrate to the United States in 1936 and reclaim her American citizenship there, with the intention of sending for her husband and the three children who still remained in Germany. Helmut had preceded her to the United States and lived with his uncle's family in Boston. As I have mentioned before and as is fairly well-known, the United States, although recognized as a nation of immigrants, did not exactly open its arms wide to these thousands of refugees who wanted so desperately to escape the Nazi terror. However, as an American citizen my aunt had a decided advantage over others, and she prepared the way for the rest of her family to follow. Lotte, the youngest child, left home in the summer of 1936, Wolfgang, the eldest, had been training as a farmer. He had no desire to go to America with his parents, but hoped for placement in an agricultural settlement somewhere. That left her husband Arno and daughter Eva. While Arno's immigration proceeded, albeit at snail's pace, Eva had no luck at all. The official at the consulate in Berlin glanced at her dull eyes and must have assumed that she was not blessed with a high IQ and that she might not be employable. Again and again Eva was subjected to IQ tests and other mental testing at the consulate in Berlin. Each time she and her father had an appoinment there, their hopes were raised. And every test she flunked. Father and daughter would return from Berlin with long faces, Eva in particular felt guilty for having failed, while her father feared that this could not continue forever and that one day he would have to give up and leave without this daughter. He finally did so, leaving for New York in the fall of 1938. Eva moved in with a woman who ran a board and care home and could use her help. There were still many relatives in Breslau who looked after her, invited her to their homes, celebrated her birthday with her, etc. But as they vanished, one by one, there were ever fewer people for her to get together with. Aunt Frieda's postcard written from Riebnig on February 17, 1942, mentions: "Today I wrote to Eva [for her birthday, which was February 25] without being able to give her anything. Trude takes care of her as much as she can." In July of that year Trude and Paul were to be sent to Theresienstadt, but they did not know that yet. In the meantime, they were seeing to it that the remaining family members still got together for coffee or tea. We do not know when Eva was deported from Breslau. It may have been in July 1942, when her Uncle Paul and Aunt Trude left. I shudder at the thought that she was taken away without any of the people she knew. She was, after all, a child, even though her age in 1942 was twenty-seven. In the eyes of the master race, Eva was undoubtedly one of those "unworthy lives" undeserving to exist, but the thought of her death among strangers, far from parents and siblings, in conditions which we know to have been inhumane and comfortless, is heartbreaking to me. Her love and kindness put to everlasting shame the people who are responsible for killing her and others like her, and her memory remains as a blessing for us who were permitted to survive the horror.

A HOLOCAUST MIDRASH[19]

One day God came to Auschwitz
Stood with the captives
On the ramp,
Wary, crouching
To avoid the blows,
The snapping curs
All around.

The prisoners cowered,
Terrified, trembling
Clutching possessions
Soothing babes,
Waiting for the decision to fall:

167

Wave to the right meant life
And yet another crust of bread,
A sip of water,
Or to the left,
To shuffle forward
In a long wavering line
To a door
From which no one returned.

Well-fed, smug guards
Stand in shiny boots
Snug, belted coats
Guns at the ready.

God looked around
At the huddled shadows
And then
At the prim, booted,
Uniformed master race.

Is this what I created?
Who took away
My imprint from their faces?
Did they? Did I?

And God turned and fled.
The dogs gave chase
But lost the trail,
For God turned into
A plume of smoke
And mingled, oh so naturally
With the smoke
Rising from the chimneys.

One day God came to Auschwitz
And fled —

CHAPTER 13

Adventures of an Autobiography

During the last vacation that Aunt Edith spent in Breslau before becoming a Carmelite, she embarked upon the project of writing a history of her family. It began with interviews of her mother, my grandmother Auguste Stein née Courant, who was 83 years old at the time. Her health was still robust, her mind sharp and clear, and she shared memories of her parents and grandparents with Edith. The year was 1933, and the idea of writing about her Jewish family had been suggested to Edith by one of her priestly mentors. Wouldn't it be a good idea, he said, to tell the public about an average middle-class Jewish family, to counteract the vicious propaganda which was being spewed forth by the government-controlled media? Show them how decent, how honest and upright your Jewish family is, and they will surely recognize the truth. It probably made sense to Edith Stein, who had just lost her teaching position in Münster, who could no longer publish her scholarly writings, was no longer invited to lecture. It might open the eyes of at least some thoughtful people, before the constant exposure to poisonous anti-Semitic attacks could infect them. Besides, Edith Stein liked the idea of writing a book about her Jewish family, because she was truly attached to them. As much as she saw their flaws and weaknesses, she loved them with all her heart. Now she was about to enter a very strict community of nuns. She would remain there for life. She would never go home, never again visit uncles and aunts, cousins or nieces or nephews. It appeared to be an ideal moment to hold fast to the pictures of past and present family tableaus. Little did she know how soon the entire fabric of the family and of the society she knew would dissolve, disintegrate and its components disperse in all directions. So many relatives would perish in the Holocaust. Capturing the past in this fashion in a family story was a wonderful idea. Very likely, my grandmother would have viewed the whole enterprise with mixed emotions. While she had not yet been told of Edith's plans to enter the Carmelite Order, she knew that changes were in the air for everyone, she was watching with dismay the gradual decline of a thriving Jewish community all around her, and she kept saying, "I never knew that there were such wicked people in the world." Doggedly she continued to go about her business, walking to the lumberyard every day, putting in a full day's labor, day after day, going home to eat a simple meal, before sitting by the window in the dim light of dusk with her knitting. The needles clicked incessantly, until it was time for bed. But sometimes, tears would well up in her eyes when she thought of the dismal situation, and then she might drop a stitch or two and have to wipe away the tears before returning to fix the problem at hand.

And so the two women sat across from each other, one asking questions and taking notes, the other searching her memories for details and anecdotes from bygone days. Ours was a large family composed of many different characters, with their quirks and idiosyncracies. And of these memories and observations, Edith wove her first chapter. From above the sofa, the grandparents, sepia-toned, in black-rimmed frames, watched the scenario, had been watching for decades, her grandmother with a serious, benevolent gaze, grandfather

170

likewise wearing an expression of attentiveness, with just a slight hint of amusement. I grew up with these faces gazing down at us, but I really knew them only from stories. They had died long before my time. It was only in 1995, that my husband and I visited Lubliniec, the small Polish town where they used to live. There we sat on the sofa that is reported to have belonged to my great grandmother Adelheid, saw her wardrobe of dark polished wood and a piano which, we were told, belonged to the Courant family. All of a sudden, in the house where the Courants once lived and had their business, I was challenged to find my connection to these people whose stories I had read in my aunt's account.

That first chapter of the book which my aunt wrote in 1933 my mother read to us children shortly after it was written. Thereafter I recall no mention of this work for decades. Presumably, Aunt Edith took this project with her when she left for Cologne. She certainly did not realize her original purpose—to communicate the story of her family to the audience for which she had originally intended it. When in 1964 we encountered this story again, much had happened in the life of this Jewish family. Grandmother Auguste Stein had died. The house in which a large part of the clan had lived, had passed into "Aryan" hands. The family Aunt Edith had described with love but also with relentless honesty had been dispersed. The book's author had been gassed in Auschwitz. We were living in America and spoke mostly English. I had grown up and had a family of my own. As for the book, it, too, had assumed a different personality than its author had planned for it. It had been conceived as the story of a family, and it had been meant to teach a lesson to counteract anti-Semitic propaganda. Instead, the book had turned out to be mostly an autobiography, although an incomplete one. It began as an account of the family but ended as one of Edith herself and, if she could have continued this work, it might have provided answers to the many questions people now ask

171

about Edith Stein, her thought processes, her spiritual path, the why and how of her conversion to Catholicism, and many more. However, the book stopped short at the point when Edith Stein celebrated with great joy her doctorate, with highest honors, and her acceptance as assistant to her admired teacher Prof. Husserl. Her entry into Catholicism would not take place for another six years. Her decision to become a Carmelite would not be made until seventeen years later. The lesson which Edith Stein had wanted to inculcate with her writing would certainly have fallen on deaf ears, even if the book had found a publisher in the Third Reich.

A number of adventures befell this manuscript before it actually was published and distributed. Edith took it with her to Cologne and was able to work on it intermittently for about one and a half years. At that point, other duties interfered, and from May 1935 until her arrival in Echt, Holland on December 31, 1938, she abandoned her work on the book. When Edith Stein left the Carmel of Cologne, she was still very much shaken by Kristallnacht, the pogrom of November 9-10, 1938, and wanted to make sure that her flight from Germany into Holland should proceed without a hitch. She therefore decided to leave the manuscript behind. Only later was she able to get this precious work back. In February 1939 she began to think about continuing the story and made cautious inquiries in Cologne about the possibility of having the manuscript brought to her in Echt. A young Marianhill missionary, Dr. Rhabanus Laubenthal, volunteered to help and took the manuscript with him by automobile. When an officer stopped and searched his car at the border, he leafed through the pages, asking "Is that your dissertation?" No more was said, and the young man was able to deliver the manuscript to its author without any mishap. From then on, Edith Stein continued work on this project, but as circumstances in Holland worsened with the German occupation, she began to fear that the discovery of her writings might endanger the community. Despite the attachment she had formed to this work and her desire to continue with it as time permitted, she buried it in a hiding place near the burial places of the Carmelite Sisters. Sr. Pia, who had helped her with this chore, reports that only a few months later, Edith changed her mind and again dug up the package containing the manuscript. Sr. Josephine Koeppel OCD has come up with an ingenious explanation for this act:

> Like Carmelites the world over, the community in Echt used woolen material to make their habits...By 1940, woolen cloth seemed nonexistent. What there was, of wool or of any other material, was reserved primarily for military use. However, through channels known to friends of the community, a large bolt of material...had been located and purchased at the black market price...In the community discussions, it became clear that Sr. Benedicta did not approve of buying forbidden material on the black market. With the same reasoning as basis, she felt it was wrong to conceal the material in a hiding place which the other nuns considered an excellent choice. A large hollow tree on the nuns' property easily accommodated the bolt of material, and it was also readily accessible for the Sister who had to make new habits for the nuns....
>
> Recalling that Edith had buried her manuscript sometime prior to the purchase of the material, we now have a very probable clue to the cause of its being dug up.
>
> When she realized that, clearly, according to her own lights, she considered concealing woolen material to be wrong, how could she any longer condone her own action of concealing a forbidden manuscript? This is an assumption, true, but how plausible![1].

We must leave it to the discerning reader to judge. Afterwards, Sr. Pia took charge of the package and hid it somewhere else. Its whereabouts remained a mystery. In 1945, Sr. Pia heard a rumor that the building of the Echt monastery was going to be used for people returning from Germany where they had been performing forced labor. To safeguard the package she had hidden, Sr. Pia retrieved it and turned it over to Father Avertanus, Provincial of the Dutch Carmelites, who eventually got it to the Husserl Archive in Brussels.[2]

It is amazing how much Edith Stein was able to accomplish in writing this book, despite the obstacles and interruptions she encountered over the years. It is clear to me that she never completed it nor whipped it into shape to the point where, in her judgment, it was ready for publication.

Prior to leaving the Carmel of Cologne, Edith Stein destroyed the will she had made as a member of the Cologne community. After she had become acclimatized to the Carmelite monastery of Echt, she executed a new will, dated June 9, 1939. It is a four-page, handwritten document, and in the left margin of the second page, the following provision is inserted, in German, by her own hand. My translation follows:

> Die Familiengeschichte bitte ich nicht zu veröffentlichen, solange meine Geschwister leben, und ihnen auch nicht zu übergeben. Nur Rosa dürfte Einblick gewährt werden und nach dem Tode der andern ihren Kindern. Über die Veröffentlichung soll auch dann der Orden entscheiden.

> As for the family history, I ask that it not be published as long as my siblings are alive, and that it should not be handed over to them. Only Rosa might have a look at it and, after the death of the others, their children . Even then the Order should decide about the question of publication.

And now begins the next act of this drama:

In May, 1948, the Province of Discalced Carmelites of the Netherlands made a contract with the Carmel *Maria vom Frieden* in Cologne concerning the publication of Edith Stein's works. They sent a letter to my mother, then living in New York, to let her know that this agreement had been reached and to request her cooperation. My mother promised to help with information, documents and pictures. In February 1960, Dr. Lucie Gelber, the curator of the *Archiv* in Brussels, acknowledged receipt of photos and a family tree, requested my mother to contribute information and documentary materials, to search her memory for anecdotal material and to write an introduction to the family history. My mother wrote this introduction which eventually was included in Edith Stein's book published under the title of *Aus dem Leben einer jüdischen Familie.*

By the beginning of 1963 preparations for the publication of this work were well under way. That spring, however, the contents of the will with its proviso concerning this book first came to the attention of the Sisters in Cologne, and they retracted their permission for the publication of this work. At this point, my parents were drawn into the fray. In a letter to my mother, the curator of the *Archiv,* Dr. Lucie Gelber, questioned the validity of the handwritten testament and urged my mother to give her permission for the publication to go forward.

> This hitherto unknown text has no legal validity whatsoever. It contains a postscript in which Edith expresses her wish that the manuscript be published only after the death of her siblings. You, dear Professor and Mrs. Biberstein, are the only surviving "siblings." For us there is no doubt that at this time, Edith would not add this codicil any more or would cross it out without hesitation...

When my mother learned of the special request contained in her sister Edith's will not to publish her autobiography during the lifetime of her siblings, she wrote to Dr. Gelber:

> I would love to know more about it. Since you and Father Romaeus are evidently the only ones who know the contents of my sister's notes, perhaps you can tell me whether they contain anything that speaks against publication during my lifetime, since, sadly, I am the only one of my siblings still living. ..Of course I have no objection against the publication *per se,* on the contrary, I eagerly await its appearance...I have full confidence that you will not do anything against Edith's wishes. Of course I am curious to hear about the further developments of this matter and hope that you will let me know.[3]

Dr. Gelber never replied, and the preparations for publication continued. Suddenly, my mother found herself squarely in the middle of a dispute between the Carmelite Sisters of Cologne and the Archivum Carmelitanum in Brussels. Threatening legal action to stop publication of this book, the Sisters turned to her and decided that there remained no other recourse but to send my mother the disputed manuscript and let her judge whether it should be published, during her lifetime, in direct violation of the author's request. On March 20, 1964, Sr. Teresia Margareta, who was in charge of the Edith Stein archives of Cologne wrote to announce that she had mailed the entire manuscript to my parents and asked that they give their opinion. Shortly thereafter, Father Romaeus also sent a copy. Whether these were identical in text is not clear.

Father Romaeus Leuven was still determined to publish, while the Carmelites in Cologne had hired a lawyer to stop publication. At this juncture, a letter was written by Bishop Queck of the Cologne diocese to the Father General in Rome with an accompanying letter by Cardinal Frings. Their concern was that the problematic passages in the book might harm the cause for the eventual canonization of Edith Stein, and he therefore urged the Father General to intervene to prevent an open break between the two parties involved in the conflict. Simultaneously, my mother received an urgent message from Sr. Teresia Margareta asking her to write to the Father General in Rome requesting that he intervene in this unsavory dispute. No one wanted to go to court, and yet the battlelines were drawn. At any rate, it was a difficult problem. On the one hand, there was the will with its clear "request" by the author. On the other, the book contained so much that was valuable and precious and that could be of great significance to its potential readers. It told the story of a Jewish family and thus fitted well into the new direction of the Catholic Church, which, after the Second Vatican Council was embarking on greater openness, on an ecumenical policy that also included a dialogue with the Jews. Therefore, even the Sisters in Cologne were ready for another look at the issue. In a long letter to the Provincial of the Netherlands, P. Christian a.S. Teresa (Heynen) Berthold, Sr. M. Amata Neyer, Prioress of the Cologne Carmel[4] explained that the cause for the canonization of Edith Stein had already begun, and that her Jewish origins played an important part, a timely part.

> The above-mentioned efforts derive an incredible timeliness from the fact that the candidate [for sainthood] is a Jew; she would be the first canonized member of the chosen people! What that signifies in relation to the past persecutions which, let us hope can be permanently consigned to the past, is surely plain to see. Moreover, we are dealing here with a *German* Jew. There is no need to stress that we Germans have more reasons than other nations to raise Edith Stein to the honor of the altars. But more than that! ...Since [Pope] John XXIII, a wholly new perspective concerning the Jewish people and its relationship to Christianity has opened up. In this connection the importance of the figure of Edith Stein can scarcely be overrated.

A copy of this letter was sent to my mother the same day, with the request that in her perusal of the manuscript, my mother also give consideration to the reasons that might speak for a publication sooner rather than later. Sr. Amata was careful to repeat that my mother was certainly entitled to require certain deletions from the text.

The irony of being asked to render a judgment on a text which, according to Edith's desires, my mother should not even be allowed to look at, did not escape her nor the Carmelite Sisters. They were conscience-stricken. To my parents the book afforded a nostalgic look into their past. They relished the vignettes of past adventures, hiking, entertainment, student life, friendships. What dismayed them were the many critical passages Edith had written about some of the family scandals and conflicts. It forced them to relive some of the conflicts concerning strained relationships between my father and Auguste Stein, his mother-in-law, and between his mother and Auguste. The marital difficulties of various relatives were described in detail, and my parents shuddered at the thought that such private matters might be on public view. They began to mark up the manuscript to indicate what in their view ought to be deleted, so that a more innocuous edition could appear. The effect was that both parties agreed to a compromise that

177

would permit publication of the book, even though it would not be the complete text. Thus the book that eventually came out in 1965 was much reduced in content. When my mother died in 1978, the way was clear for a complete text to be published, and this was done in 1985. Interestingly, the complete version that appeared then had been lying in storage ever since the great controversy and, despite the intervening two decades, no corrections or editorial changes had been made, despite new knowledge that had come to light in the meantime.

For us, the family members, this book has been a source of delight as well as dismay. It reveals a great deal not only about Edith Stein's Jewish family but also about herself. Her preoccupation with the truth led her to reveal much that caused pain to the subjects of her sketches or their offspring and might better have remained private. Too much truth is sometimes not in the best interest of all concerned. It is, after all, only in court that one must speak the truth, the whole truth and nothing but the truth. Aside from that, anyone who writes about others can only give a subjective portrait of events. The other side is not being heard. This is particularly troublesome when the other side is no longer alive to speak for himself or herself. Of those who were still alive at the time this account was published, several members of the family, including my father, felt compelled to write an account of their side of the story, for the benefit of their own children and to set the record straight. Elsewhere in this book I have referred to some of these documents, and while their inclusion does not necessarily imply that Edith misrepresented the facts, they are cited to add balance and yet another point of view.

Despite some of her harsh criticisms of family members, we owe Aunt Edith a great debt of gratitude. She captured for us a world which, by the time her book was published, had disappeared forever. That world had been destroyed by a cruel adventurer who set out to conquer the world and establish a

178

thousand year rule. His ascendancy lasted a mere twelve years, but it created such devastation that we still suffer from its effects. Edith Stein drew her portrayals with loving care. This was an act of homage to her mother, a tribute, but also a farewell, a turning away from the life she had pursued toward the silent world of the contemplative nun. It was bidding farewell to the career ambitions of academia and the security of the family home to which she was always wont to return for a refreshing pause, a resumption of contact with her roots and her home, where, in the words of Robert Frost, "when you have to go there, they have to take you in".[5]

I believe that it was Aunt Edith's firm intention to return to this work when time might permit, not only to complete the story up to the time of her writing, but also to evaluate carefully what she had written. We cannot be sure that she might have toned down some of her more troublesome passages to protect those concerned, but it is a possibility. This would also explain the postscript to her will. Obviously, when she wrote these lines, she was well aware of the precarious future she faced and wanted to be sure that she made provision for any eventuality.

This autobiographical fragment breaks off at a moment of great joy and triumph, in 1916, and Edith Stein never finished her story. Father Romaeus Leuven's book *Heil im Unheil (Well-Being in the Midst of Disaster)*[6], a sequel to her autobiographical volume, tries to complete the story of her life based on all available source material. Of necessity it does not have the sprightly immediacy of the earlier volume, but it does provide facts and events to complete the biographical sequence. It constitutes a labor of love by its author.

179

CHAPTER 14

Reading Between the Lines of the Autobiography

Edith Stein's book *Life in a Jewish Family* covers the years from her birth in 1891 to the moment she received her doctor's degree in 1916. She wanted to tell not just the story of herself but of her family, and to tell it as truthfully as possible.

A GOOD COMRADE

I really got to know Aunt Edith best through the stories of my parents. In these, Edith is remembered as a good sport, always a "good comrade". Her sense of humor, her enthusiasm for sociability and entertainment stand out. They are evident in the rhymes and humorous skits which she created for family occasions and the parodies she contributed to comic newspapers at school parties. The playlet Aunt Edith wrote for my parents' wedding, acted out by three of my older cousins, is still vividly remembered and occasionally quoted by them. Its tattered pages are still in our files, and the witty lines still evoke chuckles in those reading them today. Of these traits, relatively little shows in her autobiography. She appears rather solemn, serious, straight-laced, reluctant to let herself go. I can't help wondering whether this is the real Edith or whether it is an edited version of herself that she created in retrospect, in an effort to fit into the role of the contemplative nun that she had become by the time the major part of this work was written. If that is the case, it is rather a pity, for it hides from us the Edith Stein that the friends of her youth, the companions of her student years, knew and loved. Did she really change so radically or did she choose to emphasize those traits in herself which she believed to be superior to those earlier traits, even if less genuine? Getting to know this complex personality has been my aim in studying her autobiographical writings and even reading between the lines.

Her book illuminates several aspects of Edith Stein, her self-perception, her love of Germany, passion for learning, her attitude toward Judaism, her relationship with men, her views on women, and her love for her family, but especially for her mother. Autobiography must inevitably start out with the self. Relying as it does on memory and on as much objectivity as the author can muster, it will either result in an honest self-portrait or in a cosmetically or otherwise modified presentation.

SELF-IMAGE

Edith Stein promised to describe and criticize herself just as relentlessly as everyone else, but some readers get a different impression. Edith portrays herself as a wise, calm, serene soul, unprejudiced and therefore often consulted for advice. The violent temper tantrums of her childhood, her ambition to outshine fellow students and to show off her knowledge, tending to keep her distance from the common folk and looking down at them from the lofty perch of her own intellectual and moral superiority, she claims to have subdued in later life, citing her awareness that it is much more important to be good than to be clever.[1] Throughout, her narrative tells us how her early faults and weaknesses disappeared under the influence of her growing maturity, insight and self-perception:

181

...I had completely changed my attitude towards others as well as toward myself. Being right and getting the better of my opponent under any circumstances were no longer essentials for me. Also, though I still had as keen an eye for the human weaknesses of others, I no longer made it an instrument for striking them at their most vulnerable point, but, rather, for protecting them.[2]

When describing others, however, Edith concedes no such developmental changes. They are portrayed with all their strengths and weaknesses, static and forever unchanging.

In her description of her service as a nurse at a field hospital during the first World War, she professes her instinctive distaste for the "celebrations" taking place on the ward. When the resident physician asks her whether she will be at the party, she replies archly, "I have no intention of going. After all, I don't even know the gentleman." This was hardly the way to "win friends and influence people." It turned out badly, because Edith was a teetotaler and the party's main focus was on heavy drinking. She found it difficult to enter into the spirit of such events and won a reputation for being a bit stand-offish.

Some readers who did not know Edith Stein personally and must therefore form an opinion of her on the basis of her autobiography, may get an unfavorable impression. A great-grandniece, for example, remarked in a letter to me:

I hope you won't be offended, but I don't think I would have *liked* her very much if I had ever met her. She seems to me, from her writings and from what other people have said, to have been a very self-centered, judgmental, and intolerant individual.[3]

Edith casts herself as her mother's favorite. She refers to herself as "the final legacy from my father" and describes how her mother would go straight to Edith's room from work.[4] It does appear that Frau Auguste Stein was partial to her youngest child and, throughout her life, granted her every request and was generous with financial support. Whether as a single mother of seven she would have admitted to such favoritism, however, is questionable. She was a pretty level-headed woman, who would have done her best to be even-handed in the treatment of her children.

EDITH'S RELATIONSHIP TO MEN

In the chapter discussing her sister Erna's wedding, Edith repeatedly alludes to an inner crisis, a spiritual struggle of sorts, but since the chapter ends with the conclusion of the wedding party, we never really find out what this conflict consisted of. Various possibilities suggest themselves: If the problem was spiritual in nature, then it might have concerned Edith's growing affinity to the Christian religion and her contemplation of a break with Judaism, though this was not to happen until January 1, 1922. The other possibility is that the crisis was emotional and personal in nature.

One of the men in her life had been Hans Biberstein, although Edith was always aware that he and her sister Erna were in love and deeply committed to each other, and that she, Edith, needed to keep away. Still, the finality that came with Hans and Erna's marriage might have precipitated feelings of regret in her. There is the particularly poignant scene of the "last dance" which she describes at length, with obvious restraint and some pathos.[5] It is mentioned elsewhere in this book.[6]

Edith's relationships with members of the opposite sex were certainly flawed. She rejects harmless flirtation out of hand and admits her male fellow-students only in the role of colleagues. Any romantic involvement is out of the question. Whenever she mentions time spent in the company of a young man, she is quick to add that they were discussing philosophy. She strenuously rejects her mother's insinuation that a walk home from the university with a fellow-student and subsequent conversation while walking to and fro in front of their house might be flirtation.

Her earliest cavalier was her shy and introspective cousin Franz Horowitz, whose more extrovert twin brother Hans was fond of Erna. For a while they would squire the girls around,

183

but then the relationship loosened, because allegedly the Horowitz family believed in "the double standard,"[7] which the Steins rejected.

Several other encounters between Edith Stein and various male acquaintances were severely limited, at her preference, and led nowhere. Eduard Metis, a fellow-student in Breslau, who wrote book reviews for a newspaper, had written frivolously about an erotic topic. This upset Edith, and she subjected him to an embarrassing cross-examination to determine whether "I was dealing with a truly chaste person."[8] The poor fellow was evidently smitten with her, but she wrote him a letter which stated that

> I was accustomed to having a friendly relationship with my fellow students; I was willing to establish one with him; but he would have to relinquish any other expectations. This suggestion was accepted and, surprisingly, even though from then on we met almost daily in the university and often studied together, my new friend succeeded in suppressing whatever budding attraction he had felt.[9]

During her Göttingen years, she had several male friends and appeared to be serious about Hans Lipps. About her first impressions of Lipps, when they met as fellow-students in Göttingen in 1913, she says:

> Hans Lipps made a deeper impression on me than did anyone else. Twenty-three years old at the time, he looked much younger. Very tall, slim, but powerfully built, he had a handsome, expressive face, lively as a child's... That summer...he was unable to keep up regular attendance [at meetings of the Philosophical Society] since he was preparing simultaneously for his preliminary exams in medicine and, with a thesis on plant physiology, for his doctorate in philosophy. Studying medicine and natural science was his way of filling in the hours during which one could not philosophize...[10]

While at first Edith describes him only in terms of their relationship as fellow students, a friendship developed, and in 1915, during his military service in the First World War, Edith sent him packages.

184

One could make Lipps very happy with a field-post package. One time he acknowledged it by writing: "You have an uncanny knack for finding just what I need."
These were such diverse items as a Japanese woodcut, sometimes a few essays on the theory of relativity; more often good pralines or other sweets.[11]

No letters have been preserved from Hans Lipps to Edith Stein, and her reticence in personal matters prevented her from discussing her feelings about him, but from a letter by her friend Hedwig Conrad-Martius we know that Edith kept a photograph of Lipps on her desk and that Hedwig questioned her about it.

She loved Hans Lipps, the phenomenologist who was part of our group and who later became a full professor in Frankfurt and died as a [military] doctor in the battle of St. Petersburg [Leningrad]. I am also certain that she would have married him if he had wanted it. But he did not want to. When that was absolutely clear, I had a talk with her—concerning the photograph which, all by itself, still stood on her small desk in our Bergzabern home. I said to her that it didn't seem right to surrender totally to God and to want to dedicate oneself to Him and yet to keep on the table the picture of a man who didn't want to marry you... She was deeply affected and shortly thereafter...the picture disappeared from her desk. After all this came back to me, I believe for certain that this profound disappointment of her life contributed not inconsiderably to her conversion and baptism, yes, even to her cloistered life. And yet far be it from me to think that such a disappointment could be the sole reason for a conversion, as the world cynically might assume.[12]

Although Hans Lipps married in 1923, he and Edith remained friends, and, after the death of his wife in 1932, he proposed marriage to her. By then, Edith said, it was too late. She had found another path.[13]

We could also speculate about Edith's relationship with her friend and fellow-phenomenologist Roman Ingarden, with whom she exchanged letters over a period of more than twenty years, 1917-1938. Her letters deal mostly with the topics of philosophy and the research work of mutual friends, and contain little of a personal nature, with one exception. Her letter No. 25, dated December 24, 1917 begins with the salutation, "Mein Liebling!" (My darling.) This brief letter is followed by an uncharacteristic hiatus of more than a month of silence, or, more likely, was the only one of a series of letters which was preserved. With letter No. 26, dated January 29, the more impersonal tone and academic discussions resume. It is possible that the key to the cooling off in their correspondence is contained in some of the missing letters.

That there was at one time another dimension to their relationship is evident from a letter which Edith wrote to Ingarden on September 16, 1919, congratulating him on his marriage. In it she states:

> My friendship for you will, of course, remain unchanged. As to the other aspect which existed beside it , it would please me if you could bury it completely within yourself and also burn those letters of mine which you might still have.[14]

LOVE OF GERMANY AND NOSTALGIA FOR THE PAST

It is easy to see why those who were close to Edith during her student days enjoyed reading her descriptions of well beloved friends and fondly remembered scenes, of mountain hikes, delicacies from favorite pastry shops, etc. My mother, Erna Biberstein wrote:

> We, that is my husband and myself, have read this book with feverish eagerness [and] enjoyed parts of it very much... During this reading, our entire youth came alive for us once again.[15]

Throughout her book, Edith's enthusiasm for learning, for using her keen mind to the utmost of her capabilities, and her enjoyment of the academic milieu are plain to see. Student life in prewar Germany was totally different from that in today's America, and probably also in today's Germany. The relationship between students and their professors can hardly be imagined in an American environment. Husserl, deeply respected and affectionately referred to as "the master," is

186

vividly portrayed in these pages. Names we know from the literature come alive in Edith's descriptions.Her love of the university and her love of the German landscape are intertwined. Whenever one of her relatives or friends came to visit, Edith could think of nothing better than to take them on an excursion into the most scenic parts of the surrounding countryside, usually on foot, occasionally by train. Reading those lyrical passages, I cannot help comparing her Germany with mine, during the years when we lived there. By the time I had reached the age of reason and might have enjoyed similar adventures in the land of my birth, Hitler was in power and our lives were becoming ever more restricted. Traveling within Germany became difficult, since many hotels and inns were closed to Jews. We would find relaxation and refuge abroad, outside of Germany, where we were still welcome and where the blood-red swastika flag did not yet fly. I wonder what might have passed through the minds of my aunts, Edith and Rosa, when they traversed Germany during their train ride toward Auschwitz. Did nostalgia, with its memories of happier times in this land well up as they passed through the familiar landscape as prisoners, despised and disenfranchised, toward a baleful fate? Did Edith reflect upon the days when the world of beauty, of knowledge, of learning, lay before her like an open book which she could not wait to savor? Did she recall the patriotic fervor with which she entered upon her service as a Red Cross nurse during the First World War and her bitter disappointment when Germany lost the war, and all the proud dreams and hopes of its young people turned to regret, mourning and dejection? At that time no sacrifice for one's country had seemed too great, and now, the very country for which she had had such high hopes had disavowed her and her people and was implementing systematic plans for their destruction.

187

EDITH STEIN AND HER JEWISH HERITAGE

We know that even after becoming a Catholic, Edith Stein never denied nor sought to hide her Jewish roots; on the contrary, she was proud of them. She could no more deny her Jewish origins than her family. They were part and parcel of who she was, all through her life. And yet, a rather disturbing fact is evident from the pages of her autobiography. Edith Stein had little real knowledge of Judaism and, despite her bent for scholarship and research, she never seems to have shown any interest in making up for *this* lack in her knowledge. Why this was, we can only guess at. Edith as well as Erna, her sister and my mother, both had the same upbringing. In Judaism in those days, girls were not typically given more than a superficial Jewish education. My mother never learned Hebrew and knew little of Jewish history or liturgy. As a youngster Edith witnessed in her family an attenuated Judaism. While her mother still adhered to the customs and observances she had learned from her parents, her busy life as a head of a household and part-time mother left her little time to pay attention to making sure that her children got proper instruction in Judaic lore. On the other hand, in Judaism, a large part of observance is centered in the home, and so Edith could observe preparations for the Passover Seder, could be aware of the dietary laws and the do's and don'ts of food preparation and consumption. She witnessed some holiday observances, but about the "High Holy Days," Rosh Hashanah and Yom Kippur, she only remembers that she was kept out of school and had the leisure to read a good book. She recalls the eve of Yom Kippur, when her mother, accompanied by the older children, would attend synagogue.

> On the following morning, although Mother rose a little later than usual... she still was ahead of everyone else. Then she would go from bed to bed to bid each of us a fond farewell since she would stay in the synagogue the entire day.[16]

Edith Stein, I suspect, misunderstood this custom at which she observed her mother. It is incumbent upon Jews, before attending services on the Day of Atonement, to ask everyone for forgiveness. It is axiomatic that we cannot ask God's forgiveness until we have cleansed ourselves of any and all misdeeds toward our fellow-humans. What Edith saw her mother busy with, I submit, was the act of begging forgiveness of each of her children, perhaps without words, silently.

As the youngest member of the family, Edith got to ask the famous four questions at the Seder table, but since her teenage brothers did not conduct a very meaningful Seder, she gained little from this profoundly meaningful holiday.

Thus Edith's familiarity with Judaism was quite limited. For example, she does not know that the commandment against eating leavened bread throughout the week of Passover stems directly from the Bible (Nm 28:17) Instead she comments that these laws were "expanded with the stubborn consistency characteristic of the Jewish mind."[17] Here Edith's judgment is not based on fact. Most of Edith's relatives and Jewish friends were not religiously observant. Eduard Metis, however, was very traditional. The following passage illustrates once again her lack of understanding of some of these observances:

> One day when out walking with [Metis] I had an errand in one of the houses we passed. In the doorway I suddenly handed him my briefcase to hold while I went in. Too late it occurred to me that it was Saturday and one ought not to carry anything on the Sabbath. I found him dutifully awaiting me in the doorway. I apologized for thoughtlessly causing him to do something forbidden. "I haven't done anything forbidden," he replied quietly. "Only on the street is one not to carry anything; in the house it's allowed."
>
> For that reason he had remained in the entrance hall, taking care not to put even one foot into the street. This was an example of the talmudic sophistry which I found so repugnant. But I made no comment.[18]

Edith was simply unfamiliar with orthodox practice. Likewise, her views concerning the Jewish attitude toward death are

189

obviously based on misunderstanding and lack of knowledge. In comparing Jewish and Catholic funeral customs, Judaism comes up a failure:

> The rabbi began the eulogy. I have heard many such talks. They gave a resumé of the life of the deceased, recalling all the good things he had done, thereby rousing the sorrow of the bereaved all the more; there was nothing consoling about them. To be sure there was a prayer pronounced in solemn tones: "And when the body returns to dust, the spirit returns to God who gave it." However, nothing of faith in a personal life after death, nor any belief in a future reunion with those who died, lay behind these words. Many years later, when for the first time I attended a Catholic funeral, the contrast made a deep impression upon me. The one being buried was a well-known scholar. But no longer was mention made of his achievements or of the reputation he had won in the world. Called by his baptismal name alone, the humble soul, in all its poverty, was commended to divine mercy. But how consoling and calming were the words of the liturgy which accompanied the deceased into eternity.[19]

While there is no doubt that the two ceremonies differ, it is clear that Edith Stein was unfamiliar with the Hebrew prayers and psalms which are customarily recited at Jewish funerals. It is likely that, not knowing any Hebrew, she probably did not understand them. It is a fact that Jewish funeral observances are today recognized by many psychologists as being eminently wise and consistent with what is considered appropriate to assist the mourner in making the gradual transition from the depth of grief to a return to active life in the community and in the work place. For those readers to whom these rites and observances are meaningful, it is a sad revelation to see such a lack of understanding in one so insightful in other contexts.

Finally we find here a claim that suicide is more frequent among Jews than among the rest of the population. That does not correspond to the facts, at least in "normal" times. It is obvious that, in the years of persecution and systematic eradication of the Jewish population, when this text was written, more Jews were driven to suicide than others. These reasons are to be found not in the Jewish religion but in the diabolical nature of Nazi politics.

The conclusion could be drawn from these examples that this intelligent, intellectually curious and well-read woman somehow deliberately refrained from educating herself in Judaic studies in order to gain the knowledge necessary to render informed judgments in this area. Or perhaps my aunt felt a need to justify in her own mind her decision to leave Judaism and embrace the Catholic faith by pointing out flaws and weaknesses in the beliefs and observances of her ancestral faith.

Some people have compared Edith Stein's path to that of Franz Rosenzweig, who at one time in his life considered converting to Christianity, but was so moved by attending a Yom Kippur service that he decided to make an earnest attempt to recapture the Judaism to which he had only a slight connection and to try to recreate a bond to the religion of his ancestors. He returned to Judaism and became a renowned scholar. To this argument, feminists retort that this might have occurred in the case of Edith Stein, had she been a man. For women of her time, however, Judaism had little to offer. The limited role that Judaism traditionally assigned to women would not have satisfied Edith's hunger for profound spiritual nourishment. Jewish women today are more fortunate, especially in the United States. They are given opportunities for learning, for participating in religious services and, at least in Conservative and Reform Congregations, they are counted in the minyan, the required minimum of ten needed to constitute a quorum for prayer. They are entering the world of religious scholarship and creating new and meaningful rituals and gradually being admitted to the cantorial and rabbinical professions. From my own experience, I can testify to the fact that religious affiliation becomes much more meaningful with the opportunity to delve into the deeper layers of Jewish existence and practice.

In Edith Stein's days, things were different. Besides, her society even before the advent of National Socialism was deeply anti-Semitic. Her book shows clearly how much anti-Semitism was taken for granted and how pervasive it was. In academia, a Jew's career was severely curtailed. In most faculties, no Jew could rise beyond the rank of Assistant Professor. Baptism, however, removed this obstacle.[20]

Many Jews chose to become Christians purely for practical reasons. Only a few did so from religious conviction. Edith mentions that she owed her employment as a teacher at the municipal *Viktoriaschule* to the scarcity of available teachers during the First World War .[21] Her sister Else had been unable to get a teaching job in Prussia in peacetime and finally had to take a position in a private school in Hamburg.[22] Edith refers repeatedly to her non-Jewish appearance, and she sounded quite proud when she made a statement that no one took her to be Jewish.[23] She was quite likely unaware of the extent to which she had adopted the attitudes that prevailed in her society. Her condescending attitude toward Eastern Jews was something she shared with the majority of German Jews.

Anti-semitism and bigotry were alive and well, even before the ascent of Hitler to power. While we Jews were not happy about them, we took them for granted. And yet, nobody was prepared for what was to come: a systematized, legalized anti-Semitism, escalating by stages into deprivation of rights, economic livelihood and property and at the end "the final solution."

EDITH STEIN AND THE STATUS OF WOMEN

Let me say a few words about the status of women in the world of Edith Stein. Prussia had begun to admit women to the university in 1908. No wonder that my mother and my aunt, who entered the university in 1909 and 1910 respectively, considered themselves extraordinarily privileged and a little bit uneasy about the anomalous position in which they found themselves at the university. Not that they had any doubt about their entitlement or their ability to master the course of study they had embarked on. Erna and Edith felt secure because they had been brought up in the knowledge that women could be competent at home as well as in the business world. Their mother was a living example of that. The fact that these two girls were the first in their family to attend university was yet another proof that their mother supported the idea of education for women fully, with her mind and with her money. However, quite often they found themselves the target of surprised glances from the males, the professors and especially the alumni. The rowdiness of the fraternity parties was all too well known; heavy drinking was de rigueur. Among the issues of the day were women's rights.

> At that time we were all passionately moved by the women's rights movement. Hans [Biberstein] was a rara avis among the male students: he often spoke up for equal rights for women as radically as any of us. We often discussed the issue of a dual career [for women, namely marriage and profession]. Erna and our two girl friends had many misgivings, wondering whether one ought not to give up a career for the sake of marriage. I was alone in consistently maintaining, that I would not sacrifice my profession on any account. If one could have predicted the future for us then! The other three married but, nevertheless, continued in their careers. I alone did not marry, but I alone assumed an obligation for which, joyfully, I would willingly sacrifice any other career.[24]

The status of women seemed to be at a crossroads. On the one hand, women were fighting for equal rights, but yet emancipation had its limits. In a course Edith taught for young women in the Academic Branch of the Humboldt-Society for Adult Education, it became obvious that the female students preferred segregated classes to coeducation and a woman teacher to a male teacher. "They expressed their relief at being rescued from taking the course with the others; they would have felt so awkward in the presence of the young men."[25]

193

There was an even greater problem with women studying away from home. They had to find lodgings, and in Göttingen, where Edith went next, the landladies were often unwilling to accept female tenants.

Edith was fortunate. Her landlady was a young, friendly woman.

> When one was looking for lodgings, it was very embarrassing to have a grouchy face appear at a crack in the door only to mumble a few words of rejection. So we had been lucky indeed.[26]

And finally she tells of a female student whose mother accompanied her to Göttingen to take care of her daughter and provide for her. The father had to remain at home alone all year long.[27]

For the reader today, it seems strange that these young women could not fix their own meals but had to eat at student lunch tables. At most, they prepared their own breakfast. While Edith lived for a time in the apartment of her cousin Richard Courant, a cleaning woman came every day to service the coal furnace and cook breakfast for the young student.[28] How times have changed!

*　　*　　*

A final word about this autobiographical book. Who, in the final analysis, is the heroine of this book? Is it Edith or is it her mother Auguste? Many readers have argued that the portrait of this mother, of almost biblical dimensions, stands out. She presides over this family, providing, dominating, cajoling, rejoicing and grieving. She is at times manipulative, jealous and demanding, but she is beloved by all her children and grandchildren.

It may perhaps be appropriate to conclude this essay about this family history with a quotation from my father's letter addressed to his children, because it reveals yet another perspective on her autobiographical account:

194

When I think about the reasons for Edith's treatment of intimate family matters in the way she did, particularly in the knowledge that this book might be published, I can only conclude that , despite all her feeling of security which she displays, she had a profound guilt feeling toward her mother concerning the choice of her path.

She who revels in the conviction that she was her mother's favorite, had to be aware that none of her children-in-law, who, without exception, were regarded as "bad," and none of her siblings had caused their mother so much disappointment and grief as she, whose every wish had been granted (regardless of whether she was, in fact, her favorite or not). The family history, begun in September 1933, when she was about to enter religious orders, she wrote, not just as a tribute but really as a glorification of her mother.[29]

Some passages saddened those whose family conflicts appeared all too open to scrutiny, but all in all, we are glad to have this authentic document from the hand of an aunt whom we all loved and revered.

CHAPTER 15

In the Spirit of
Catholic – Jewish
Understanding

My awareness of being Jewish dates back to first grade. The school I attended was a public elementary school, but under Catholic auspices.[1] A crucifix hung in every classroom, and the schoolday began with prayers. One day, my teacher called me to her desk and told me that my parents had requested that I be dispensed from making the sign of the cross and joining in class prayers. I was somewhat puzzled, but no further explanation was offered. Obediently, I henceforth refrained from crossing myself and participating in prayer. I was also excused from Religion classes, while all my classmates learned about the Christian religion. Our classroom was decorated with many colorful scenes from the life of Jesus, of which I knew nothing.

Not long after that I became friends with another little girl in my class. Gretel was gentle and good-natured. One day, she met me after Religion class, dissolved in tears. When I asked the cause of her distress, she told me that she had just learned that the Jews killed Jesus. She knew that I was a Jew, and she did not want to believe that I was such a wicked person. Naïve as I was, I tried to comfort her by saying that I knew nothing about this, that neither I nor anyone in my family had ever killed anyone. I reassured her that she must have misunderstood something.

I remember this incident, because it was my first encounter with anti-Jewish teaching in the framework of Christian religious instruction. Fortunately this kind of instruction ended more than forty years later with the changes introduced since the Second Vatican Council (1962-1965).

By age seven, I had entered a Jewish religious school, together with my younger brother. We were taught beginner's Hebrew, some Biblical history, Jewish customs and holiday observances. Learning about Judaism and participating in home observances soon gave us some understanding of how we differed from most of our neighbors.

Years later I found out that my parents were particularly intent on seeing to it that we children received a thorough Jewish education, because they felt that my aunt Edith, who had become a fervent Catholic, might have followed a different path, had she been given a thorough grounding in her Jewish heritage.

While I was not eager to spend afternoons in school studying Judaic subjects, I was to find myself deeply grateful in later years at having been coerced into Jewish studies and at having received a rather thorough grounding, even though our home observances were rather slim. We lit Sabbath candles, but our main Jewish event took place on the first Seder[2] night, when the whole clan gathered in the large *Saal*[3] in Grandmother's house. My father recited the Haggadah[4], and a sumptuous meal with all the ceremonial foods was served. Whenever I recall our extended family as it was before the advent of Nazism and the dispersion of Jews to the four corners of the world, it is the Seder gathering that rises most vividly before my eyes.

197

In our neighborhood, Jews were a very small minority. Since my brother and I had black hair and olive complexions, we stood out as being distinctly different from our schoolmates. Anti-Semitic slurs were often flung at us by passing youngsters. We pretended not to hear these words and never responded. From an early age it was drummed into us that we must never do anything to make ourselves conspicuous. The theory appeared to be that, if we did not stand out, if we behaved correctly, minded our own business and did our best in every respect, no one could find fault with us or harm us. Knowing now how all those well brought-up, well-behaved Jewish children fared under the Hitler regime, one cannot help but feel the sharp irony of it all.

In the spring of 1933 my aunt Edith was dismissed from her teaching position in Münster. Thinking about her future, she conceived a bold plan: She would seek an audience with Pope Pius XI and plead with him to issue an encyclical denouncing anti-Semitism. Her efforts were nobly, but perhaps a bit naively, conceived. She was informed that this was a "Holy Year" and for that reason the crowds making pilgrimages to Rome were so large that there was no prospect for Edith Stein to be received by the pope in a private audience.[5] The best she could hope for was to be admitted as part of a small group. She decided that that would not serve her purpose, and instead sent a letter to the pope in which she set forth her plea in detail. As far as I know, this letter is still among the sealed documents of the Vatican; we only have her own description of this incident.

> I know that my letter was delivered to the Holy Father unopened; some time thereafter I received his blessing for myself and for my relatives. Nothing else happened. Later on, I often wondered whether this letter might have come to his mind once in a while. For in the years that followed, that which I had predicted for the future of the Catholics in Germany came true step by step.[6]

In her desire to bring about a better understanding between Christians and Jews, Edith Stein was ahead of her times. Sadly enough it took the horrors of the Shoah, the Holocaust, to bring about the far-reaching changes that began with Pope John XXIII's decision to convene the Second Vatican Council in 1962 and the profound changes that flowed from that event. Edith Stein was just one of the millions who were killed because they were Jews. In her plea to Pope Pius XI, she spoke for the people from whom she was descended. But other statements still show her as a pre-Vatican II Catholic. In her will, she declares her intention to atone for the unbelief of the Jewish people, and in a conversation with her mother, just before her entry into the Carmelite Order, she counters her mother's words, that it's possible to be devout as a Jew, with the words, "Certainly, if one has not come to know anything else."[7] The implication is clear: The "something else" is something better.

At this point I must strongly deny the authenticity of one of those "legends" about Edith, in which she is said to have used her Catholic breviary to recite prayers while attending Jewish religious services with her mother. My mother Erna always stated that "Edith would never have done that. She was far too decent and respectful for that."

Neither Edith Stein's letter nor the arguments of other more prominent personages could impel the pope to issue an encyclical condemning anti-Semitism. It is often said that Pius XI's encyclical *Mit brennender Sorge,* published in 1937, was a response to Edith Stein's plea, but this document was not issued until four years later and did not mention the Jews. When the pope charged Father John LaFarge, an American Jesuit, to draft an encyclical on the topic Edith Stein had mentioned in the spring of 1933, it was long in the making. The encyclical was never issued, and the final draft did not become known until 1997. It has only recently been revealed how circuitous the road toward bringing forth this document really was, and the actual text shows that the prejudices of the past had not

199

been shed by its authors and are still present in this text. Father Jan Nota[8], who located and analyzed the text of the draft of *Humani Generis Unitas,* the unity of the human race, found so much outdated theology in this document that he said, "God be praised that this draft remained only a draft!"[9]

The Church has come a long way since that time. The Second Vatican Council (1962-1965) brought the Church into the modern era by facilitating contact among the various branches of Christianity and encouraging innovative thinking. Vatican II also opened a new relationship with the Jews through the famous document *Nostra aetate,* the Declaration on the Relation of the Church to Non-Christian Religions. Only with this document, published October 28, 1965, under the direction of Cardinal Augustin Bea, did the Catholic Church reject "persecution against whomsoever it may be directed." Msgr. John M. Oesterreicher, in an assessment of the Church's progress, twenty-five years after the publication of *Nostra aetate,* says:

> We - Christians as well as Jews —... must learn to understand how the other thinks and feels, moves and acts. We must never impute false motives to one another, never cease to respect each other. We must not forget that the Conciliar Declaration is an instrument of peace, a singular opportunity, given us by God, not to be lost.[10]

With his facility in many languages and his willingness to travel the globe, even now, at the age of 78 and in ill health, Pope John Paul II has managed to build bridges where hitherto seemingly unbridgeable gulfs existed. The pope listens to Jewish concerns. Wherever he travels, he usually arranges a meeting with representatives of the local Jewish community. When controversy arose concerning the establishment of a Carmelite monastery adjacent to the death camp of Auschwitz, the pope saw to it that this monastery was moved.

In 1993, he established diplomatic relations between the Vatican and Israel. And in 1994, he sponsored a concert at the

Vatican, commemorating the Shoah. Earlier on, in 1986, Pope John Paul II made a historic decision; he paid a visit to the great synagogue of Rome, the first pope ever to go there. On that occasion, he clearly condemned anti-Semitism. He addressed the Jews as "our elder brothers". He even recalled the deportations of the Jews of Rome during the Holocaust. These actions and statements of the present pope have been welcomed in Jewish circles. They stand in sharp contrast to the policies of the Vatican during the rise of National Socialism.

On July 20, 1933, the Vatican concluded a concordat—a kind of mutual non-interference agreement—with the Hitler government, signed by Eugenio Pacelli, then Secretary of State to the Holy See, the later Pope Pius XII. I remember clearly that the news of the signing of the concordat between the Vatican and Germany had a devastating impact on Germany's anti-Nazis and especially Jews. At that time the Vatican could have taken a stand against Nazi ideology and against Hitler's program of bigotry and belligerence, without any risk at all. In fact, as the spiritual leader of the Roman Catholics in Germany, the pope could have swayed a large segment of the German population to recognize the incompatability of National Socialist programs and policies with the moral principles of the Church. Instead, this pact boosted the prestige of this disreputable new German chancellor in the eyes of the world.

By the time war broke out in September 1939, effective intervention may have become much more difficult than it would have been between the years 1933 and 1939, the six preceding years, when Hitler's power grew and his evil program was being put into practice step by step. During those years, Pope Pius XI and his successor, Pope Pius XII could have accomplished a great deal.

While much evidence has been collected concerning the role Pius XII played during the war years in which the Nazis carried out the fiercest persecution of the Jews, not all the pertinent documents are yet available to examine all the facts and come up with an objective report. Therefore, rather than belaboring past history, let us look at important steps being taken by the Vatican today.

On May 26,1994, during talks held in Jerusalem, the Church announced that it was preparing a draft of a document acknowledging the Church's role in fostering centuries of anti-Semitism and in failing to stop the Holocaust.

It was to be drafted by a committee consisting of German and Polish bishops and its working title was "Anti-Semitism, Holocaust and Church." This 14-page document was eleven years in the making and was eventually released on March 16, 1998 under the title "We Remember: A Reflection on the Shoah.". While it expresses remorse for the failings and transgressions of individual Catholics, it appears to absolve "the Church" as an institution from any guilt in the Holocaust. It also draws a distinction between the "anti-Semitism" of the Nazis and the "anti-Judaism" found in the general society. While it states that "the Shoah was the work of a thoroughly modern, neo-Pagan regime", it admits that anti-Jewish teachings and preachings had, for centuries, contributed toward laying the foundation on which Nazi doctrines could blossom. The initial Jewish reaction was mixed. However, Cardinal Cassidy, president of the Vatican Commission for Religious Relations with the Jews, in a speech before the Amerian Jewish Committee in Washington, DC on May 15, 1998, gave his "reflections" on the above-mentioned statement.[11] He clarified some points and urged his listeners not to take this document in isolation from those already issued by the episcopal conferences of several European countries nor from the many statements by Pope John Paul II. Those who are working diligently in an ongoing effort toward conciliation, such as Rabbi James Rudin and Dr. Eugene Fisher[12], stress the fact that this document, while imperfect, represents an important step along the road to greater openness. It gives the lie to Holocaust deniers and can serve as a teaching tool. It ends with the following inspiring message:

> We pray that our sorrow for the tragedy which the Jewish people has suffered in our century will lead to a new relationship with the Jewish people We wish to turn awareness of past sins into a firm resolve to build a new future in which there will be no more anti-Judaism among Christians or anti-Christian sentiment among Jews, but rather a shared mutual respect, as befits those who adore the one Creator and Lord and have a common father in faith, Abraham.[13]

In general, however, Jewish leaders express disappointment and dismay, noting particularly that the Catholic clergy in Germany, France and Poland have issued statements that go much further in accepting responsibility for the failures of the Church in Nazi times than this document issued by the Vatican. Jewish voices are calling for an opening of the Vatican archives to permit access to documents pertinent to the Holocaust, so that the truth can be ascertained.

I inherited my involvement with Jewish-Catholic dialogue years ago, from my mother. As the only surviving sibling of Edith Stein, she had maintained a vast international correspondence with many persons interested in Edith Stein. Some were scholars, others merely devotees, and others, who were themselves converts from Judaism to Catholicism saw in Edith a kindred spirit. To many people, Edith Stein stood for a sort of fusion between Judaism and Christianity. After my mother died in January 1978, at the age of almost 88, her interfaith correspondence and her Edith Stein connections fell into my lap, and I have been dealing with this heritage ever since. As I found myself called upon to respond to queries from many different directions, both Christian and Jewish, I had to clarify my own thinking as well as keep informed on this topic and keep abreast of progress and change.

Prior to the beatification of Edith Stein, I wrote an article for the New York Times Magazine[14] in which I spoke about my aunt, her relationship to her Jewish family and the attitude of that family toward her conversion to Catholicism and taking the veil of Carmel. It became clear to me then that the chief focus of debate about her today is this question: Is Edith Stein a figure for reconciliation or a figure of controversy in Catholic-Jewish dialogue and an impediment to the effort at rapprochement? It is the question with which the various Edith Stein Societies in different parts of the world wrestle, and it comes up every time the name of Edith Stein is in the news. Even among Edith Stein's relatives this question has been hotly debated and argued. My cousin Gerhard Stein, who became a Protestant when he married, insisted that

> just as it is told that Jesus sacrificed his life for the sins of mankind, so Edith, according to reports, went consciously to her death by gas as a sacrifice for her beloved Jewish people. Portents for her destiny are her birth on the Day of Atonement, the Jewish observance of reconciliation with God for all trespasses, and her death on the yearly day of mourning for the destruction of the temple in Jerusalem (Tisha b'Av)...[15]

Gerhard Stein believed that Edith Stein could symbolize to the world the Jewish people who perished in the Holocaust. There is something troubling to those of us who are Jewish in viewing someone who turned away from Judaism and embraced Christianity as a symbol for the Jews. In her own family, Edith was only one of four siblings who fell victim to the Nazis. In addition, there is the problem with the concept of Edith going to her death "for her people." The death of Jesus is considered by Christians to be a redemptive death. By his sacrifice, Jesus atoned for the sins of the people. In contrast, my aunt Edith was killed alongside millions of Jews. Her suffering and death could not save the others. It was a death she did not choose, could not choose and could not have avoided. It was a death which did not stop the killing or give a religious meaning to the slaughter. It was a fact that Edith Stein died in solidarity with "her people". Even though she had left the Jewish fold, she was finally, in an ironic twist, reunited with them in death. She was resigned to that fate, but she had no control over it. It was rather due to the Nazis'definition of who is a Jew. It was because she was born Jewish, of Jewish parentage, that she became a "Martyr in Auschwitz".

Prior to Edith Stein's beatification, my brother Ernst Ludwig Biberstein put it as follows:

> Edith pursued her emigration [from Holland] literally till the last moment in evident hope of being rescued. Thus one can hardly speak of a longing for a sacrificial death. And a sacrifice for whom? She is quoted, apocryphally, perhaps,... as having said , "We are going for our people." What does this "for" mean? Does that mean, "in place of?" That hardly corresponds to the facts. Or, "in behalf of them?" For their atonement and salvation , perhaps,because they remained obstinate in their unbelief? Is that the basis for her martyrdom and beatification? In that case, I would have to distance myself from it quite decisively. In that case, I could not allow myself to take part in this ceremony. That would be an almost blasphemous debasement of the sacrifice of the millions who, for the sake of their faith, *al kiddush hashem,* i.e. for the sanctification of God's name, went, like her, to a bestial death. [16]

The occasion of Edith Stein's beatification in Cologne on May 1, 1987 offered many opportunities to debate these matters. Of Edith Stein's nephews and nieces who were present, not all were Jewish. Cousin Gerhard Stein has already been mentioned. Cousin Werner Gordon, who was then living in Colombia, South America and who has since died, was married to a Catholic and was the father of a large clan, all of whom were reared as Catholics. I had always assumed that he himself had converted, but after his death we learned that he had requested to be buried in a Jewish cemetery. His family respected his wishes.

On the occasion of the beatification of our aunt Edith Stein, very diverse views about the significance of the event and of the symbolic meaning of Edith Stein were revealed in our discussions. What was, however, most heartwarming about this family reunion was our feeling of family closeness. After it was all over, we continued the discussion and debate. We did not all suddenly agree, but we had found a way to communicate and remember our common familial bond. This year, as many of us prepare to attend Edith Stein's canonization in Rome, we remember the uplifting experience of May 1987 and are already looking forward to renewing our family bonds and continue the interrupted dialogue.

In a small way, the family of Edith Stein mirrors the family of humankind. Just as the family of Edith Stein could come together in this setting, despite our different backgrounds and beliefs, so Jews and Christians can come together in an atmosphere of peace and good will, to open a dialogue, to reach some understanding and find a way to bridge our differences. In the confines of one extended family, we find various religious allegiances represented. At times our discussions can become quite heated, but we respect each other's right to differ. After the political upheavals that scattered us in all directions, we refuse to allow ideological or religious differences to tear us apart. Our basic entity as family must remain a unifying principle.

My contacts with inquiring individuals and groups have been quite revealing and stimulating. My conversations with Christian friends and acquaintances on topics of Jewish-Christian relations have given me new and varied insights. Everywhere we have visited Edith Stein-related places, we have been most cordially received. My visits to various Carmelite monasteries have also contributed to my understanding of the life of my aunt after she entered this order. We have visited Carmelite convents in Germany, Poland, and various American cities, and we have found great diversity among them. The most traditional is probably the Carmelite monastery in Wroclaw, where the nuns still sit across from their visitors, separated by a grille, with black veils covering their faces. The most untraditional is the monastery in Reno,

Nevada, where the Sisters typically wear bluejeans and sweatshirts. But these are all external signs. Their work and their dedication are more alike than different, and their lively interest in Edith Stein is the same everywhere. They are eager to meet someone who really knew their Carmelite sister and can give them a unique glimpse of her as she was in her family environment. We rarely discuss politics with the nuns, but most of them are not as cut off from the outside as one might think. They know what is happening in the world, and, unlike the Carmelites in my aunt Edith's time, they are permitted visits to family members in time of illness or death.

I have maintained close contact with the various Edith Stein organizations here and abroad and found a great deal of cross-fertilization from these contacts. The Cologne Carmel *Maria vom Frieden,*[17] the monastery to which Edith Stein belonged, maintains the definitive archival collection of documents and artifacts pertaining to the life and work of Edith Stein. Its curator, Sr. M. Amata Neyer OCD, is probably the closest to a walking encyclopedia on Edith Stein in the world. The *Edith-Stein-Carmel*[18] in Tübingen, Germany, also holds a large collection of Edith Stein material and is fostering the study and dissemination of Edith Stein-related research. Sr. Waltraud Herbstrith, the present Prioress, is a prolific writer and lecturer on the subject of Edith Stein.

The Dominican Sisters of St. Magdalena in Speyer[19], where Edith Stein taught from 1923 to 1931, have established a small museum in the room which Edith Stein occupied during those years. They have assembled books, documents and mementos and receive many visitors who are eager to seek out one of the places where she lived and worked. The nuns of St. Magdalena hold their famous erstwhile faculty member in fond memory and high honor. A beautiful, well researched book, written by Maria Adele Herrmann OP, portrays the years that Edith Stein spent in Speyer and serves as a tribute and documentation of this phase of Edith Stein's life.[20]

In a somewhat diferent vein, there is a unique memorial to Edith Stein in Lambrecht/Pfalz. This exhibit is the creation of a Carmelite Brother Toni Braun, who has collected a large array of artifacts, books, and mementos from his pilgrimages along the path of Edith Stein's life from Wroclaw (Breslau) to her birthplace, to Auschwitz, where she was murdered, as well as from encounters with her friends and relatives. Encouraged by his Carmelite monastery in Mainz, Fr. Braun established his Edith Stein Memorial in his parental home, the Toni Schröer-Haus, and conducts tours for individuals or groups in an effort to spread the knowledge of Edith Stein's life and work and to promote her message of love, faith, and better understanding among nations and religions.[21]

In the United States, there is the *Edith Stein Center*[22] at Spalding University in Louisville, Kentucky, which was founded by Sr. Mary Catharine Baseheart in 1991. Its growing library and distinguished lecture programs are dedicated to Edith Stein and to Catholic-Jewish dialogue.

Several Edith-Stein societies have sprung up in this country and abroad: The Edith Stein Guild[23], based in New York, was founded in 1955 by twelve people who came together because of their interest in improving Jewish-Catholic relations. Their aim was to disseminate knowledge of Edith Stein, to help Catholics of Jewish origin to adjust to their new religion and to further understanding between Catholics and Jews. The organization today has more than three hundred dues-paying members and a mailing list of over one thousand. Many of its original members are still active and enthusiastic participants in its work. In 1988, the Guild bestowed its annual Edith Stein Award on Sr. Josephine Koeppel OCD and on me, for our "efforts to create an atmosphere of greater understanding between Catholics and Jews through [our] writings."

Other societies that are dedicated to the veneration and study of the life and works of Edith Stein are:

Edith-Stein-Society of Wroclaw, Poland (*Towarzystwo im. Edyty Stein*), founded in 1989.[24] This group has taken as its purpose the spreading of information about the life and work of Edith Stein, to promote her canonization, and to work for better relations between Catholics and Jews and between Poles and Germans. After surmounting many obstacles, the society has acquired the former home of the Stein family in Wroclaw, which had belonged to Edith's mother Auguste Stein and after her death to Auguste's children, and is establishing there a center for Christian-Jewish and Polish-German dialogue, a museum and library, a place for lectures and research. The house is currently being renovated and restored.

We have visited Wroclaw twice in recent years and each time have been in contact with the Society. During our most recent visit in 1997, the board of the organization expressed its frustration concerning its earnest attempts to establish a closer connection with the Jewish community of Wroclaw, only to meet with rebuffs. They believe that, in this instance, the name Edith Stein does not work to build bridges but instead puts obstacles between them and the Jewish group. When they approach the Jewish community in the name of Edith Stein, an attempt at proselytizing is suspected. The difficulty, of course, is that a Jewish convert to Christianity cannot be viewed as a role model for the Jewish community. We therefore encouraged the Edith Stein Society to try to find projects of mutual interest and benefit on which to work cooperatively with the Jewish community rather than to invite the Jewish group to their meetings. Meeting on neutral ground and working toward common goals, might yield some positive results.

The *Edith Stein Society of Lubliniec, Poland*[25], closely connected with the larger organization in Wroclaw, was founded June 27, 1991. It maintains a permanent exhibit on Edith Stein and her ancestors who lived in this town when it was still known by its German name Lublinitz. The stated purposes of this society are the same as those of Wroclaw. Lublinitz was the home of Edith's grandparents and the birthplace of Edith's mother and most of her older siblings. It became Polish after the First World War and plebiscite of 1921.

The *Edith Stein Society of Germany (Edith-Stein-Gesellschaft Deutschland)* was founded April 30, 1994 and is based in Speyer.[26] Its purpose is to connect the many groups in Germany who occupy themselves with Edith Stein, to enable them to communicate and exchange information. It aims to promote the veneration of Edith Stein, to disseminate her message and the witness of her life and work; to further research in philosophy, theology, religion, organize symposia, pilgrimages, Christian-Jewish dialogue, and to promote Polish-German understanding. The society issues an *Edith Stein Jahrbuch* (Yearbook), with scholarly articles on various aspects of her work and life and related topics. There may be other groups or organizations dedicated to the life and works of Edith Stein, but I am not aware of them.

My contacts with understanding and sincere people, who are serious about wanting to enrich their knowledge and to add to mine by mutual exchange of ideas have been gratifying. On the other hand, I have occasionally encountered others, who are really only intent upon convincing me of the superiority of their own faith and show by their actions that they have misunderstood the meaning of dialogue, as they really want to pursue a missionary agenda toward the Jews.

Christians and Jews have already come a long way toward closer rapprochement and better understanding, but our work is not finished. We must learn about each other's beliefs and ideology with open minds and mutual respect, conceding to each other the right to be different, to worship in our own ways.

One final word about forgiveness: The Jewish people cannot forgive the perpetrators of the Holocaust or those who stood silently by. The survivors cannot forgive the death of the victims. We can listen to the *mea culpas* of those who are truly repentant and leave forgiveness to God. If we examine our past and admit our mistakes honestly, we can go forward confidently and work together for common goals. And with God's blessing we can go about the task of *tikkun olam*, repairing the world.

EDITH STEIN'S LITERARY WORKS

A listing of the works of Edith Stein is reproduced by permission of the Edith Stein Guild from *Documents Concerning the Life and Death of Edith Stein*, by Jakob Schlafke, NY, Edith Stein Guild, 1984. English equivalents of the titles have been added in brackets. Where English translations exist, relevant bibliographic information is also given.

1917 *Zum Problem der Einfühlung*. Inaugural-Dissertation, Halle, 1917. Reprint, Kaffke, 1980.
On the Problem of Empathy, 3d rev. ed., transl. by Waltraut Stein, Washington, DC, ICS, 1989. Collected works of Edith Stein, v. 3)

1922 *Jahrbuch für Philosophie und Phänomenologische Forschung*.
Bd. V "Individuum und Gemeinschaft."
BD. VII "Psychische Kausalitat"
(Yearbook for Philosophy and Phenomenological Research.
v. V "Individual and Society."
v. VII "Psychic Causality.")

1924 Bd. VIII *Untersuchung über den Staat.*
(Investigations Concerning the State)

1928 Übersetzung: Newman, *Briefe und Tagebücher bis zum Übertritt zur Kirche,* Bd. I der Gesammelten Werke. München, Theatiner-Verlag, 1928.
(Translation: John Henry Newman, *Letters and Diaries up to his Conversion to the Church,* v. I of Collected Works.)

1929 *Die Phänomenologie Husserls und die Philosophie des hl. Thomas von Aquin*. Halle, Niemeyer.
Jubiläumsaugabe für Husserl.
(The Phenomenology of Husserl and the Philosophy of St. Thomas Aquinas. Jubilee edition for Husserl.)

1931 *Des hl. Thomas von Aquino Untersuchungen über die*

Wahrheit. Zwei Bände. Neu herausgegeben von Herder, 1952.
(*The Investigations Concerning the Truth,* by St. Thomas Aquinas. 2 vols. New edition by Herder, 1952).

1931 *Akt und Potenz.* Umarbeitung 1934-36 in *Endliches und Ewiges Sein, Versuch eines Aufstiegs zum Sinn des Seins.* Edith Stein, *Gesammelte Werke,* Freiburg, Herder, 1962, v. 2.)
(*Action and Power.* Revision 1934-36 into *Finite and Eternal Being, an Attempted Ascent to the Meaning of Being.*

1932 *Über Glaube, Wissen und Erkennen.* Unveröffentlichtes Fragment. Loeven, Husserl-Stein Archiv.
(*Concerning Faith, Knowledge and Cognition.* Unpublished fragment.)

1932 *Ethos der Frauenberufe.* In Edith Stein: *Gesammelte Werke,* Freiburg, Herder, v. 5, p. 1)
Ethos of Women's Professions, in Edith Stein: *Essays on Woman,* tr. by Freda Mary Oben, 2d ed., rev., Washington, DC, ICS, 1996. (*Collected Works,* v. 2., p. 43.)
Probleme der Frauenbildung. In Edith Stein: *Gesammelte Werke,* Freiburg, Herder, 1959, v. 5, p. 93.
Problems of Women's Education, in Edith Stein: *Essays on Woman,* tr. by Freda Mary Oben, 2d ed., rev., Washington, DC, ICS, 1996. (*Collected Works,* v. 2., p. 147.)
Lebensgestaltung im Geiste der hl. Elisabeth. In Edith Stein: *Gesammelte Werke,* v. 11, p. 27 (*Shaping Life in the Spirit of St. Elizabeth)*
Eingliederung der Frau in das Corpus Christi Mysticum. Beruf des Mannes und der Frau nach Natur und Gnadenordnung. In Edith Stein: *Gesammelte Werke,* Freiburg, Herder, 1959, v. 5, p. 17.

The Separate Vocations of Man and Woman According to Nature and Grace, in Edith Stein, *Essays on Woman*, tr., by Freda Mary Oben, 2d ed. *rev.*, *Washington, DC, ICS, 1996. (Collected Works*, v. 2, p. 59)

1932 *Wege zur inneren Stille*, Monatsbrief für die Societas Religiosa.
Neu veröffentlicht im *Lebensbild einer Philosophin und Karmelitin, Edith Stein*, von Schw. Teresia Renata de Spiritu Sancto. 6. Auflage, 1952, p. 100-104. (*Paths to Inward Silence*. Newly published in *Life of a Philosopher and Carmelite, Edith Stein*, 6th ed., 1952)

1932 *La phénomenologie*. The German and French text of the discussions which took place in Juvisy may be found in *Journées d'études de la société thomiste*. Juvisy, Editions du Cerf, 1932.

1932 *Aufgabe der Frau als Führerin der Jugend zur Kirche. In Edith Stein: Gesammelte Werke*, Herder, 1959, v. 5, p. 189.
The Church, Woman and Youth, in Edith Stein, *Essays on Woman*, tr. by Freda Mary Oben, 2d ed. rev., Washington, DC, ICS. 1996. (*Collected Works*, v. 2, p. 237)

1932 *Die ontische Struktur der Person und ihre erkenntnistheoretische Problematik*. Fragment. Unpublished manuscript of her lectures at the German Institute for Scientific Pedagogy, Münster. The handwritten manuscript may be found in the Archives of the Carmelite Moanstery in Cologne)
In Edith Stein: *Gesammelte Werke*, Freiburg, Herder, 1962, v. 6, p. 137.) (*The Structure of Being of the Person and Its Problematics Concerning Its Theory of Knowledge*. Fragment.)

1932-*Theologische Anthropologie*. Fragment. Unvollendetes
1933 Manuskript nicht mehr gehaltener Vorträge, Loeven, Husserl-Stein Archiv. (*Theological Anthropology*.

Fragment. Unfinished manuscript of lectures which were never delivered.)

1933 *Übersetzung der Briefe des Areopagiten. Himmlische Hierarchie, kirchliche Hierarchie.* Unveröffentlichtes Manuskript.
(*Translation of the letters of the Areopagite. Heavenly Hierarchy, Ecclesiastical Hierarchy.* Unpublished manuscript*).*

1934 *Das mystische Sühneleiden des hl. Johannes vom Kreuz.* Unveröffentlicht. Loeven, Husserl-Stein Archiv.
(*The Mystical Passion of Expiation of St. John of the Cross.* Unpublished.)

1934 *Teresia von Jesus.* Konstanz, Kanisius Verlag. In Edith Stein: *Gesammelte Werke,* Herder, 1987, v. 11, p. 40.)
Love for Love: The Life of St. Teresa of Jesus. In Edith Stein, *The Hidden Life,* tr. by Waltraut Stein, Washington, DC, ICS, 1992, p. 29 (*Collected Works,* v. 4)

1934 *Die hl. Teresia Margareta Redi.* Würzburg, Rita Verlag. Übersetzung der Zeremonien der Einkleidung und des Schleierfestes im Orden Unserer Lieben Frau vom Berge Karmel.
(*St. Teresa Margareta Redi;* Translation of the clothing ceremony and the feast of the veil in the Order of Our Lady of Mt. Carmel.)

1935 *Geschichte der Familie Stein.* Husserl-Stein Archiv. *(History of the Stein Family)* Published as: *Aus dem Leben einer jüdischen Familie* (Edith Stein: *Gesammelte Werke, v.7,* Complete edition, Freiburg, Herder, 1985.) *Life in a Jewish Family,* Washington,DC, ICS. 1986. English transl. by Josephine Koeppel, OCD).

1936 *Gebet der Kirche.* In Edith Stein: *Gesammelte Werke,* Herder, 1987, v. 11, p. 10.) *Prayer of the Church.* Edith Stein, *The Hidden Life,* tr. by Waltraut Stein

Washington, DC, ICS, 1992, p 7 (*Collected Works, v. 4*)

1937 *Mutter Franziska Esser. Eine deutsche Frau und grosse Karmelitin.* Veröffentlicht in *Die in Deinem Hause wohnen,* von P. Eugen Lense. Verlagsanstalt Benziger u. Co.
(*Mother Francisca Esser. A German Woman and a Great Carmelite.* Published in *They That Live in Thy House.*)

1937 *Missae et Officium in honore B.V.M. sub titulo: Regina Pacis.* Ein Exemplar Maschinenschrift mit Handkorrekturen von Edith Stein im Archiv des Klosters der Karmelitinnen zu Köln.
(*Masses and Office in Honor of the Blessed Virgin Mary, Under the Title : Queen of Peace.* One copy in typescript with hand-written corrections by Edith Stein in the Archives of the Carmelite Monastery in Cologne,.)

1938 *Pater Andreas vom hl. Romuald OCD.* Aachen, Karl Gatzweiler. Veröffentlicht in *Stimmen vom Karmel.* Bamberg, Jahrgang 1939
(*Pater Andreas of St. Romuald OCD.* Published in *Voices from Carmel. 1939*)

1938 *Sancta Discretio.* Handgeschriebenes Manuskript im Archiv des Klosters der Karmelitinnen in Köln.
(*Holy Distinction.* Handwritten manuscript in the Archives of the Carmelite Monastery in Cologne.)

1938 Persönliche Widmungen (Personal Contributions):
Mein Göttinger Semester. Von Dom Raphael Walzer zur Verfügung gestellt für *Das Lebensbild einer Philosophin und Karmelitin, Edith Stein,* von Schw. Teresia Renata de Spiritu Sancto.
(*My Semester in Göttingen.* Made available by Dom Raphael Walzer for the *Biography of a Philosopher and Carmelite, Edith Stein,* by Sr. Teresia Renata de Spiritu Sancto.)

"Wie ich in den Kölner Karmel kam". Ein Beitrag zur Kölner Chronik." Veröffentlicht in *Lebensbild einer Philosophin und Karmelitin, Edith Stein,* von Schw. Teresia Renata de Spiritu Sancto. (Also in Edith Stein: *Wie ich in den Kölner Karmel kam,* ed. by M.A. Neyer, Echter, 1994) "How I Came to the Cologne Carmel". In Edith Stein: *Selected Writings, ed.* by S. Batzdorff, Springfield, IL , Templegate, 1990, p. 13.

1939 *Die Hochzeit des Lammes.* In: Edith Stein: *Gesammelte Werke,* Freiburg, Herder, 1987, v. 11, p. 127) *The Marriage of the Lamb.* In Edith Stein: *The Hidden Life, tr.* by *Waltraut Stein,* Washington, ICS, 1992, p. 97 (*Collected Works,* v. 4).

1941 "Wege der Gotteserkenntnis". Veröffentlicht in *Tijdschrift voor Philosophie. 8.* Jahrgang, 1946. Loeven, Husserl-Stein Arachiv "Ways to Know God." Published in *Tijdschrift voor Philosophie,* v. 8, 1946.) Published in English, tr. by Rudolph Allers, in *The Thomist, v. 9 # 3, July, 1946,* and as a booklet *Ways to Know God,* ed. by Josephine Koeppel, OCD, Edith Stein, Guild, 1981.

1941- *Die Kreuzeswissenschaft.* Unvollendet. Edith Stein
1942 arbeitete an diesem Werk bis zu ihrer Gefangennahme am 2. August, 1942. Loeven. Published as Edith Stein *Gesammelte Werke,* 3d ed., Freiburg, Herder, 1983. *Science of the Cross.* Unfinished. Edith Stein was at work on this project when she was arrested on August 2, 1942.) Translation by Sr. Josephine Koeppel, Washington, DC, ICS, 1998.

1942 "*Selbstbiographie.*" Handgeschriebenes Manuskript im Husserl-Stein Archiv. in Loeven. ("*Autobiography.*" Handwritten manuscript.)

To date, Edith Stein's works have appeared in seventeen volumes, edited by Lucy Gelber and Fr. Romaeus Leuven ODC and later, Lucy Gelber and Fr. Michael Linssen.

I. *Kreuzeswissenschaft: Studie über Johannes a Cruce* 3d ed. Freiburg, Herder, 1983
(Science of the Cross; a Study of John of the Cross)
English translation by Sr. Josephine Koeppel OCD. Washington, DC, ICS, 1998

II. *Endliches und ewiges Sein.*
Versuch eines Aufstiegs zum Sinn des Seins 2d ed. Freiburg, Herder
(Finite and Eternal Being, an Attempted Ascent to the Meaning of Being)

III. *Des Hl. Thomas von Aquino* I. Teil 1952
Untersuchungen über die Wahrheit, Freiburg, Herder
(St. Thomas Aquinas's Investigations Concerning Truth, Part 1)

IV. *Des Hl. Thomas von Aquino* II.Teil 1955
Untersuchungen über die Wahrheit, Freiburg, Herder
(St. Thomas Aquinas's Investigations Concerning Truth, Part 2)

V. *Die Frau:* 1959
Ihre Aufgabe nach Natur und Gnade, Freiburg, Herder
(Woman: Her Task According to Nature and Grace.
English trans. by Freda Mary Oben, *Essays on Woman,*
2d rev. ed., Edith Stein: *Collected Works,* v. 2
Washington, DC, ICS 1996

VI. *Welt und Person* 1962
Beitrag zum christlichen Wahrheitsstreben, Freiburg, Herder
(World and Individual; a Contribution to Christian Striving for Truth)

VII. *Aus dem Leben einer jüdischen Familie* 1985
Das Leben Edith Steins: Kindheit und Jugend,
Edith Stein: Complete 2d ed., Freiburg, Herder

Life in a Jewish Family, transl. by Josephine Koeppel
OCD: Edith Stein: *Collected Works*, v. 1, Washington,
DC, ICS,   1986
VIII.*Selbstibildnis in Briefen 1916-1934*   I. Teil 1976
(Self-Portrait in Letters, 1916-1934. Part I) Freiburg,
Herder
IX. *Selbstbildnis in Briefen 1934-1942*   II. Teil 1977
(Self-Portrait in Letters, 1934-1942. Part 2) Freiburg,
Herder
English transl. by Josephine Koeppel OCD, *Self-
Portrait in Letters, 1916-1942*, Edith Stein: *Collected
Works*, v. 5, Washington, DC, ICS   1993
X.   *Heil im Unheil*   1983
Das Leben Edith Steins: Reife und Vollendung, Freiburg,
Herder
*(Salvation in the Midst of Evil, The Life of Edith Stein:
Maturation and Completion)*, Freiburg, Herder
Written by Fr. Romaeus Leuven, OCD, this volume
is based on Edith Stein's notes, letters and on documents
and reports contributed by reliable witnesses and friends
of E.S.
XI. *Verborgenes Leben; Hagiographische Essays,
Meditationen, Geistliche Texte*,
Freiburg, Herder,   1987
The Hidden Life; Essays, Meditations, Spiritual Texts,
tr. by Waltraut Stein, Washington, ICS, 1992.
XII. *Ganzheitliches Leben; Schriften zur Religiösen Bildung*,
Freiburg, Herder,   1990
*Integrated Living; Writings Concerning Religious
Education.*
XIII. *Einführung in die Philosophie.*
Freiburg, Herder,   1991
Introduction to Philosophy.
XIV.*Briefe an Roman Ingarden, 1917-1938.*
Freiburg, Herder,   1991
Letters to Roman Ingarden, 1917-1938.

SOURCES CONSULTED IN THE PREPARATION OF THIS BOOK

This list includes only published material, although the author used letters and unpublished essays from her own personal files.

Batzdorff, Susanne, M.: "A Martyr in Auschwitz,"
  New York Times Magazine, April 12, 1987
"Breslau," *Encyclopedia Judaica,* Jerusalem,
  Keter, 1972, v. 4, p. 1353.
Czerwinski, Janusz: *Breslau, Schlesische Metropole an der
  Oder,* Berlin, RV Verlag. 1993
Gay, Ruth, *The Jews of Germany; a Historical Portrait,*
  New Haven, Yale univ. pr., 1992.
Herbstrith, Waltraud, OCD, ed. *Never Forget: Christian
  and Jewish Perspectives on Edith Stein,* Washington,
  DC, ICS 1998
Herrmann, Maria Adele, OP: *Die Speyerer Jahre von Edith
  Stein, (Edith Stein's Years in Speyer),* Speyer,
  Pilger-Verlag, 1990.
Juden in Preussen; ein Kapitel deutscher Geschichte, ed.
  Bildarchiv Preussischer Kulturbesitz, Dortmund,
  Harenberg Kommunikation, 1981. 3d ed., 1982
Kölner Selig-und Heiligsprechungsprozess der Dienerin

Gottes Teresia Benedicta a Cruce (Edith Stein), Cologne, 1962,

Koeppel, Josephine *Edith Stein, Philosopher and Mystic*, Collegeville, MN, Luturgical press, 1990

Lagiewski, Maciej: *Breslauer Juden, 1850-1944*, (*The Jews of Breslau*), Wroclaw, Muzeum Historyczne, 1996.

Leuven, Romaeus, OCD, *Heil im Unheil*, Freiburg, Herder, 1983 (Edith Stein, *Gesammelte Werke*, v. 10, 1983

Neyer, Maria Amata OCD: "Die Familie Stein in Lublinitz" ("The Stein Family in Lublinitz"), in *Edith Stein Jahrbuch*, 1997, Würzburg, Echter, 1997

Neyer, Maria Amata, OCD, "Edith Steins Werk 'Endliches und ewiges Sein'; eine Dokumentation" [Edith Stein's work *Finite and Eternal Being;* a Documentation"] In *Edith Stein Jahrbuch 1995*, Würzburg, Echter, 1995

Oesterreicher, John M.: "A New Beginning: Reflections on *Nostra aetate* after 25 years." In Ecumenical Trends, March 1991

Okolska, Danuta: *Edith Steins Spuren in Breslau*, Wroclaw, Arboretum, 1997

Passelecq, Georges & Bernard Suchecky, *The Hidden Encyclical of Pius XI*, NY, Harcourt, 1997.

Posselt, Teresia Renata de Spiritu Sancto, OCD: *Edith Stein*, NY, Sheed & Ward, 1952

Reflections: The Vatican Statement on the Shoah, by Edward Idris Cardinal Cassidy, Pres. Vatican Commission for Religious Relations with the Jews. Address to the American Jewish Committee, Washington, DC, May 15, 1998.

Salter, Mark & Gordon McLachlan: *Poland*. London, The Rough Guides, 1994

Scheyer, Ernst: *Breslau so wie es war*, Düsseldorf, Droste Verlag, 1969

Scholem, Gershom: *From Berlin to Jerusalem; Memories of My Youth,* New York, Schocken, 1980

Stein, Edith: *Briefe an Roman Ingarden, 1917-1938.* Freiburger, Herder, 1991, *(Edith Stein, Gesammelte Werke, v. 14)*

Stein, Edith: *Life in a Jewish Family,* Washington, DC, ICS, 1986 (Edith Stein, *Collected Works,* v. 1)

Stein, Edith: *Self-Portrait in Letters,* ICS, Washington, DC, 1993 (Edith Stein, *Collected Works,* v. 5)

Stein, Edith: *Selected Writings,* ed. by Susanne M. Batzdorff, Springfield, IL, Templegate, 1990.

Stein, Edith: *Studentin in Göttingen, 1913-1916,* Göttinger Bibliotheksschriften, 1993

We Remember: A Reflection on the Shoah, by Edward Idris Cardinal Cassidy, President, Vatican Commission for Religious Relations with the Jews, the Most Reverend Pierre Duprey, Vice President, and The Reverend Remi Hoeckmann, O.P., Secretary, March 16, 1998.

FOOTNOTES

Prologue

1 "Susel" was an affectionate pet name derived from my name "Susanne".

2 Stein, Edith: "How I came to the Cologne Carmel," in Edith Stein, *Selected Writings*, Springfield, IL, Templegate, 1990, p. 27.

Chapter 1

1 Salter, Mark & Gordon McLachlan : *Poland*. London, The Rough guides, 1994, p. 382.

2 Stein, Edith: *Life in a Jewish Family*, Washington ICS, 1986, p. 168.

3 Czerwinski,Janusz: *Breslau, Schlesische Metropole an der Oder,* Berlin, RV Verlag, 1993, p. 50. According to another source, Ernst Scheyer, *Breslau so wie es war,* Düsseldorf, Droste Verlag, 1969, p. 10, it did not receive this name until its centenary in 1911.

4 Czerwinski, Janusz: *op. cit. p. 49-50.*

5 Brahms had received an honorary doctorate from the University in 1879 and subsequently composed this piece as a token of appreciation, dedicating it to the University of Breslau.

6 Stein, Edith: *op. cit.*, p. 204-205.

7 *Ibid.*, p. 171-172.

8 *Ibid.*, p. 84.

9 *Ibid..*, p. 192.

Chapter 2

1 Lagiewski, Maciej: *Breslauer Juden, 1850-1944, (The Jews of Breslau),* Wroclaw, Muzeum Historyczne, 1996, illus.28.

2 *Encyclopedia Judaica*, v.2, p. 1353.

3 *Ibid.*, p. 1354.4 Gay, Ruth, *The Jews of Germany; a historical portrait*, New Haven, Yale univ. pr., 1992, p. 127.

5 *Ibid*, p. 129

6 *Ibid.*, p. 131.

7 *Juden in Preussen; ein Kapitel deutscher Geschichte*, ed. Bildarchiv Preussischer Kulturbesitz, Dortmund, Harenberg Kommunikation, 1981. 3d ed., 1982, p. 157.

8 *Ibid.*, p.162-163.

9 College for the Study of Judaism.

10 When we visited Wroclaw in June, 1997, members of the Jewish Community there told us that during the High Holy Days of 1996, services were held in a portion of the women's gallery of this building, which was in relatively safe condition. Although the Jewish community of Wroclaw has an estimated number of 200, on that occasion about six hundred people streamed into the ruin of the synagogue to participate in religious services. It caused a sensation and attracted the attention of the news media.

11 Lagiewski, Maciej, op. cit. p. 9.

12 The Seminary building , located on Wallstrasse 1b was torn down after the second World War.

13 Stein, Edith: *Selected Writings*, Springfield, IL, Templegate, 1990, p. 28. Although my grandmother did not usually attend services at that synagogue, on that

particular day, one of the most eminent and brilliant scholars on the faculty of the Seminary, Rabbi Yitzhak Heinemann (1876-1957) gave a sermon, which, my grandmother believed, would be of interest to Edith as well.

14 Gay, Ruth: *op. cit.* p. 152.

15 *Juden in Preussen, op. cit.*, p. 278-279.

16 Scholem, Gershom: *From Berlin to Jerusalem; memories of my youth.* New *York, Schocken, 1980, p.27.*

17 *Ibid.*, p. 25-27.

18 Alfred Dreyfus, 1859-1935, an officer in the French army, falsely accused of high treason and sentenced to life imprisonment. Anti-Semitism was at the root of the process, and only through the vigorous defense mounted by Emile Zola was a reversal of this miscarriage of judgment accomplished and Dreyfus rehabilitated.

19 *Juden in Preussen*, p. 257.

20 *Ibid..*, p. 338.

21 *Ibid*, p. 342.

Chapter 3

1 The demise of this Jewish community is mentioned briefly in an article by Karol Jonca "Deportations of German Jews from Breslau, 1941-1944 as described in eyewitness testimonies, Yad Vashem Studies XXV:p.281, as follows: 'The Gestapo deported Jews from Langendorf [Wielowies] near Gleiwitz on June 8, 1942."

2 See footnote 1 above.

3 Buchen, Julie, "Erinnerungen an meine Kindheit und an das Elternhaus, meinen Neffen und Nichten gewidmet, um ihnen ein Bild des damaligen Familienlebens zu bieten." ("Reminiscences of my childhood and the home of my parents, dedicated to my nephews and nieces, to give them an idea of family life at that time." (Typescript, 1920), p. 4

4 *Haggadah*, lit, *The Telling*, refers to the narration of the Exodus story read on the Passover Seder.

5 The actual date was August 2, 1871.

6 Buchen, J., *op. cit.*, p. 17-18.

7 Stein, Edith: *Life in a Jewish Family*, ICS, 1986, p .38.

8 *Ibid.*, p. 39.

9 *Ibid*.

10 Neyer, Maria Amata OCD: "Die Familie Stein in Lublinitz"("The Stein Family in Lublinitz"), in *Edith Stein Jahrbuch, 1997, Würzburg, Echter , 1997, p.385-402. Much of the story of the Siegfried Stein Family in Gleiwitz and Lublinitz is reconstructed in this article, based on research by Johann Fikus,Sr., in Lublinitz.*

11 Stein, E. *op. cit.*, p. 27-28.

12 *Ibid.*, p. 29. This surprising sentence is misquoted in Edith Stein's book as "Lord, send us only as much as we can bear" but my mother used to quote the other version and assured me that that is how her great grandmother, Ernestine Burchard, nee Prager used to say it.

13 *Ibid.*, p. 33-34.

14 Neyer, A.: *op. cit*

15 Nowadays, this house which is being restored and renovated and has become the property of the Edith Stein Society of Wroclaw, is generally referred to as "The Edith Stein House."

16 Neyer, *op. cit.*, p. 387-398.

Chapter 4

1 This interview took place in Los Angeles on Dec. 30, 1977, and my mother died on January 15, 1978.

2 Stein, Edith: *Life in a Jewish Family*, Washington, DC ICS, 1986, p. 41.

3 *Ibid*. p. 17.

4 *Ibid.*, p. 44

5 The word "Jitschl" which was applied to Edith as a young child was, according to my mother's explanation, a part Upper Silesian/part Polish dialect word for a small child.

6 Stein, Edith, *op.cit.*, p. 54.

7 *Ibid.*, p.14. Biberstein, Erna: "Reminiscences, 1949."

8 Stein, Edith, *op. cit.*, p. 50.

9 *Ibid.*, p. 63.

10 *Ibid.*, p. 115

11 *Ibid.*, p. 78. The school year began at Easter.

12 *Ibid.*, p. 66.

13 *Ibid.*, p. 55-56.

14 Buchen,Julie, "Erinnerungen an meine Kindheit und an das Elternhaus, meinen Neffen und Nichten gewidmet, um ihnen ein Bild des damaligen Familienlebens zu bieten." ("Reminiscences of my childhood and the home of my parents, dedicated to my nephews and nieces, to give them an idea of family life at that time," (Typescript, 1920), p. 3.

Chapter 5

1 Stein, Edith *Life in a Jewish Family*, Washington, ICS, 1986, p. 90.

2 *Ibid,* p. 92

3 *Ibid,* p. 139

4 *Ibid,* p. 96

5 *Ibid.*, p. 148

6 Herbstrith, Waltraud, OCD, ed. *Never Forget,* Washington, ICS, 1998, p. 72.

7 Stein, Edith, *Life in a Jewish family*, p. 148.

8 *Ibid.*, p. 159.

9 *Ibid.*, p. 141.

Chapter 6

1 Biberstein, Ernst Ludwig, sketch titled *Erinnerungen an Tante Rosa, (Memories about Aunt Rosa)*, unpublished, p. 2. (My translation into English)

2 Stein, Edith, *Life in a Jewish Family*, ICS, 1986, p. 38

3 *Ibid.*, p. 30-31.

4 *Ibid.*, p. 38.

5 *Ibid.*, p. 41.

6 *Ibid.*, p. 45-46.

7 Stein, Gerhard, Letter to Sr. Josephine Koeppel, dated October 28, 1984, p. 3.

8 Stein, Edith, *op cit.*, p. 46.

9 Sachs, Lotte, née Stein in a letter to Susanne Batzdorff, dated Nov. 15, 1997.

10 Neyer, Maria Amata, OCD, "Edith Steins Werk 'Endliches und ewiges Sein'; eine Dokumentation" ["Edith Stein's work *Finite and Eternal Being*; a Documentation"] In *Edith Stein Jahrbuch 1995, Würzburg, Echter, 1995, p.320.*

Chapter 7

1 Stein, Edith, *Life in a Jewish Family*, p. 176-177.

2 Stein, Wolf S., Letter dated March 1, 1993.

3 Biberstein, Ernst Ludwig : Unpublished sketch entitled. "The house on Michaelisstrasse 38," p. 2-3.

4 *Ibid.*, p. 1-2.

5 Teresia Renata de Spiritu Sancto [Posselt]: Edith Stein, NY, Sheed & Ward, 1952, p. 3.

6 *Ibid.*, p. 4

7 Okolska, Danuta:*Edith Steins Spuren in Breslau, Arboretum, Wroclaw, 1997, p. 13.*

8 According to a document issued by Katasteramt [land registry] of April 29, 1939 registering the transfer of property from Auguste Stein, née Courant, to the new owner Jandel.

9 Biberstein, E.L.: *op. cit.* p. 6.

10 Okolska, *op. cit.*, p. 13.

11 Stein, Edith: *Aus dem Leben einer jüdischen Familie, Herderverlag, 1965, p. 53.* The pages following an event that occurred in 1903 were omitted, and when the story resumed with the purchase of the house, it appeared that this purchase happened in 1903.

Chapter 8

1 Stein, Edith: *Life in a Jewish Family*, p. 117.

2 *Ibid.*, p. 117

3 *Ibid.*, p. 237. The German text has "seelische Kämpfe", the translator in the ICS edition rendered it as "spiritual conflicts". It could relate to Edith Stein's struggle over her religious conflicts but, on the other hand, it might be translated as "emotional conflicts" and refer to a romantic relationship. Since we will never know for sure, I prefer to leave the interpretation to the reader.

4 *Ibid.*, p. 237.

5 *Ibid.*, p. 63-64.

6 *Ibid.*, p. 205-206.

7 *Ibid.*, p. 121-122.

8 *Ibid*, p. 120.

9 *Ibid.*, p. 119-120.

10 Biberstein, Hans: Untitled essay addressed to his son and daughter in response to the description of himself and his mother in the book *Life in a Jewish family*. Undated, this essay must have been written in 1964, shortly before publication of the first German edition of Edith Stein's book *Aus dem Leben einer jüdischen Familie. p. 2.*

11 *Ibid*, p. 1.

Chapter 9

1 Stein , Edith, *Life in a Jewish Family*, Washington , DC, ICS, 1986, p. 239.

2 *Ibid.*, p. 218.

3 *Ibid.*, p. 240.

4 *Ibid.*, p. 242 Today, such a plaque can be seen outside the house Lange Geismarstrasse 2, in which Edith Stein lived as a philosophy student. The text reads: Edith Stein, Philosophin, 1913-1916.

5 *Ibid.*, p. 16 Erna Biberstein née Stein:"Reminiscences," New York, 1949.
6 *Ibid.*, p. 220. In the original German:
Manches Mädchen träumt von Busserl,
Edith aber nur von Husserl.
In Göttingen da wird sie sehn
Den Husserl leibhaft vor sich stehn.
7 *Ibid.*, p. 249.
8 Schuhmann, Karl:"In Göttingen wird nur philosophiert...Man spricht nur von Phänomenen," In *Edith Stein; Studentin in Göttinger, 1913-1916, Göttinger Bibliotheksschriften, 1993, p. 106.*
9 Stein, Edith, *op.cit.*, p. 274.
10 *Ibid.*, p. 63.

Chapter 10
1 Biberstein, Ernst Ludwig, "Erinnerungen an Edith Stein," in Herbstrith, Waltraud, ed.: *Edith Stein, eine grosse Glaubenszeugin, Plöger, 1986, p. 130-131.[Translation by S.M. Batzdorff]*
2 Gordon, Ilse, "A great, exceptional human being," in *Never Forget*,ed. by Waltraud Herbstrith, Washington, DC, ICS, 1998, p. 71.
3 *Ibid.*, p. 71-72.
4 Stein, Edith, *Life in a Jewish Family*, Washington, DC, ICS, 1986, p. 104-105.
5 Stein, Edith, *op cit.*, p. 86.
6 Gertrude Stein née Werther was the wife of Uncle Paul, the eldest of Edith's siblings. She was usually referred to as "Trude."
7 Stein, Edith, *op. cit.*, p. 86.
8 Stein, Gerhard, Letter to Sr. Josephine Koeppel, dated Oct. 28, 1984, p.3-4.
9 This anecdote seems to contradict one contained in the earliest biography *Edith Stein*, by Sr.Teresia Renata Posselt, Edith Stein, Sheed & Ward, 1952, in which she cites "Frau [Katharina] Ruben, Edith's godchild" who says that, even though "everyone expected her to get the prize... instead of her it was given to Martha Ritter, the head of our class." P. 8 However, Mrs. Ruben recalls that this incident took place in 1905, on the 100th anniversary of Schiller's death, whereas Gerhard Stein cites Schiller's 150th birthday, which would have taken place in 1907. It is therefore conceivable, though unlikely, that, while Martha Ritter was awarded the Schiller prize in 1905, a similar prize went to Edith two years later.
10 Stein, Gerhard "Radio talk about my experiences with my aunt Edith Stein," March 31, 1987, p.1. Note discrepancy between this version and that described in his letter, Footnote 7 above.
11 Sachs,Lotte Stein , Letter dated Nov. 10, 1997, p. 2.
12 Stein, Edith, *op. cit.*, p. 218-219.
13 Sachs, Lotte Stein, Letter in answer to my query, Nov. 10, 1997. It appears that Lotte's father visited his sister Edith in the Cologne Carmel on October 14, 1938, on his way to America.
14 Bjørnssen, Bjørnstjerne: Ein fröhlicher Bursch, Insel Bücherei # 199. It is inscribed, in German, "To dear Lotte, as a memento of her visit to Carmel."
15 *Kölner Selig- und Heiligsprechungsprozess der Dienerin Gottes Teresia Benedicta a Cruce (Edith Stein), Cologne, 1962, Paragraph 45, Item 4, p. 34.*
16 *Ibid.*, Paragraph 83, Item 13-14, p. 65.

Chapter 11

1 Diminutive for "Mother" in Silesian dialect

2 At that time, the medical specialty qualifying examinations were relatively new and by no means common.

3 Friedhof Cosel is located on ul. Lotnicza (Flughafenstrasse), in the northwestern part of Wroclaw. My maternal grandparents are buried in the older cemetery, located on ul. Slezna (Lohestrasse), in the south of the city.

4 Our son Jonathan Richard Batzdorff and his wife

5 Our oldest son Ronald Albert Batzdorff, his wife Nan and children Hector and Heloise.

Chapter 12

1 Stein, Edith, *Life in a Jewish Family*, Washington, DC, ICS, 1986, p. 39.

2 *Ibid.*, p. 43

3 Stein, Gerhard, Letter to Sr. Josephine Koeppel OCD, dated October 28, 1984, p.5-6.

4 Biberstein, Ernst Ludwig, "Four Letters Across," an unpublished essay, October 25, 1995.

5 The *Sh'ma* is a brief statement of faith in one God, the best known prayer in Jewish liturgy.

6 Stein, Paul, Postcard to Dr. Goldstein, an intermediary in Switzerland, dated July 17, 1942.

7 Stein, Paul, Letter to his son, Gerhard Stein in the United States, dated October 17, 1940.

8 Stein, Gertrude, Letter to her son, dated February 9, 1941.

9 *Ibid.*

10 Stein, Paul, letter to his son and family dated March 31, 1941.

11 Kaddish, refers to the "Mourners' Kaddish, a praise to God, spoken by mourners

12 *Hillul Hashem*, means blasphemy.

13 Biberstein, Ernst Ludwig, *Erinnerungen an Tante Rosa* , p. 2.

14 Postcard by Frieda Tworoger née Stein to her sister Rosa in Echt, Holland, dated February 17, 1942.

15 E. L. Biberstein, *op. cit.*, p. 3.

16 Stein, Edith, *Self-Portrait in Letters*, ICS, p. 308 (Letter No. 300 to Mother Petra Brüning, April 16, 1939).

17 Barbara van Weersth was a relative of Mother Johanna van Weersth, prioress of the Carmelite monastery of Beek , Netherlands, with whom Edith Stein corresponded. 18 Stein, Edith, *Self-Portrait in Letters, p. 321-322 (Letter No. 312)*

19 A *midrash* is an imaginative interpretation of Scripture, revealing meanings beyond the literal one.

Chapter 13

1 Koeppel, Josephine, *Edith Stein, Philosopher and Mystic, Collegeville, MN, Liturgical Press, 1990, p. 165.*

2 Stein, Edith, *Life in a Jewish Family*, Washington, DC, ICS, 1986, p. 463.

3 Letter from Dr. Erna Biberstein to Dr. Lucie Gelber, May 19, 1963

4 Letter dated April 22, 1964.

5 Frost, Robert, "Death of the Hired Man."

6 Leuven, Romaeus, OCD, *Heil im Unheil*, Freiburg Herder, 1983.

Chapter 14

1 Stein, Edith, *Life in a Jewish Family*, p. 142.

2 *Ibid.*, p.234-235.

3 Strope, Julia, replying to a questionnaire by Susanne Batzdorff in Autumn, 1987.

4 Stein, Edith, *op. cit.*, p. 73.

5 *Ibid.*, p. 237.

6 A fuller account of this incident is found in Chapter 8 of this book.

7 The principle of granting greater sexual freedom to men than to women.

8 Stein, Edith, *op. cit.*, p. 211-212.

9 *Ibid.*, p. 211.

10 *Ibid.*, p. 254.

11 *Ibid.*, p. 370.

12 Letter by Hedwig Conrad–Martius to Montsignor Oesterreicher, in: Waltraud Herbstrith, ed. *Never Forget*, ICS, 1998, p. 238-239

13 Koeppel, Josephine, *Edith Stein, Philosopher and Mystic,* Collegeville, MN, Liturgical Pr., 1990, p. 56.

14 Stein, Edith, *Briefe an Roman Ingarden, 1917-1938.* Freiburg, Herder, 1991, Letter # 65, p. 119. translation by Susanne Batzdorff.

15 Letter to Sr. Teresia Margareta OCD, dated April 1, 1964.

16 Stein, Edith, *Life in a Jewish Family*, p. 72.

17 *Ibid.*, p. 69. My translation is closer to the original text than that of Sr. Josephine Koeppel, retaining its slightly pejoratve meaning.

18 *Ibid.*, p. 212.

19 *Ibid.*, p. 81.

20 This stands in direct contrast to the later Nuremberg laws. Under these regulations, a Jew was Jewish if his grandparents had been Jewish. Thus a baptized Jew still remained Jewish.

21 Stein, Edith, *Life in a Jewish Family*, p. 391.

22 *Ibid.*, p. 394.

23 *Ibid.*, p. 343.

24 *Ibid.*, p. 123.

25 *Ibid.*, p. 204.

26 *Ibid.*, p. 240.

27 *Ibid.*, p. 291.

28 *Ibid.*, p. 304.

29 Biberstein, Hans, *Letter to His Children, Susanne[Batzdorff] and Ernst Ludwig [Biberstein]*, p. 22.

Chapter 15

1 In Germany, the administration of many public elementary schools was subcontracted to either the Protestant or Catholic Church.

2 *Seder* is the designation given to the first night of Passover. It is observed in the home with a reading of the Passover story and a festive meal.

3 "Saal" means a room suitable for large gatherings or festivities.

4 *Haggadah,* lit, *The Telling,* refers to the narration of the Exodus story read on the Passover Seder.

5 1933 was considered the 1900th anniversary year of the death of Jesus Christ. Thus this year was singled out for pilgrimages to Rome and other holy places.

6 Stein, Edith, *Selected Writings*, Templegate, 1990, p. 17.

7 *Ibid.*, p. 28.

8 Nota, Johannes Hille, SJ, 1913-1995, born in Holland, taught philosophy at various universities in Europe, the United States and Israel. His last teaching position was at Brock University in Ontario, Canada. Prof. Nota met Edith Stein while she was in the Carmelite monastery in Echt. This encounter brought him in contact with Edith Stein's philosophy and was a significant impulse toward a lifelong engagement in Jewish-Christian dialogue.

9 Passelecq Georges & Bernard Suchecky, *The Hidden Encyclical of Pius XI* , Harcourt, 1997, p. 12.

10 Oesterreicher, John M.,"A new beginning: Reflections on *Nostra aetate* after 25 years." In *Ecumenical Trends*, March 1991, p. 46.

11 "Reflections: The Vatican Statement on the Shoah," by Edward Idris Cardinal Cassidy, Pres. Vatican Commission for Religious Relations with the Jews. Address to the American Jewish Committee, Washington, DC, May 15, 1998.

12 Dr. Eugene Fisher, Secretariat for Ecumenical and Interreligious Affairs, Washington, DC.

13 "We Remember: A Reflection on the Shoah," by Edward Idris Cardinal Cassidy, President, the Most Reverend Pierre Duprey, Vice President, and The Reverend Remi Hoeckmann, O.P., Secretary, March 16, 1998, final page.

14 Batzdorff, Susanne M., "A Martyr in Auschwitz," *New York Times Magazine*, April 12, 1987, p. 52.

15 Stein, Gerhard, Article contributed to the Radio Station Deutsche Welle in Cologne on April 3, 1987, p.4. [G. Stein is in error concerning Edith's death on Tisha b'Av. In 1942, the Ninth of Av, a Jewish day of mourning for the destruction of the Holy Temple in Jerusalem and for other disasters in Jewish history, fell on July 23. The lunar calendar, by which Jews reckon their festivals, varies from the Gregorian calendar. Hence the observance of Jewish feast and fast days varies from year to year, according to the secular calendar. Thus, while the Ninth of Av always occurs during July or August, it did not coincide with the death date of Edith Stein.]

16 Biberstein, Ernst Ludwig, Statement addressed to Radio Station Deutsche Welle, April, 1987, p. 3.

17 Edith Stein Archiv
Karmel Maria vom Frieden
50676 Cologne
Vor den Siebenburgen 6
GERMANY

18 Edith-Stein-Karmel
72070 Tübingen
Neckarhalde 64
GERMANY

19 Dominican Convent St. Magdalena
D67346 Speyer
Hasenpfuhlstrasse 32, Germany

20 Herrmann, Maria Adele, OP: *Die Speyerer Jahre von Edith Stein, (Edith Stein's Years in Speyer)*, Speyer, Pilger-Verlag, 1990.

21 Edith Stein Gedenkstätte
Toni-Schröer-Haus
Hauptstrasse 93
67466 Lambrecht/Pfalz

GERMANY
22 Edith Stein Center for Study and Research
Spalding University
851 South Fourth Street
Louisville, KY 40203
John R. Wilcox, Curator
23 Edith Stein Guild
210 West 31st St.
New York, NY 10001-2876
24 Towarzystwo im. Edyty Stein
ul. Nowowiejska 38
PL.50-315 Wroclaw, POLAND
Dr Marian Lukaszewicz, President
25 Towarzystwo im. Edyty Stein, Oddzial w. Lublincu,
ul. E. Stein 2
42-700 Lubliniec, POLAND
Maria Burek, Secretary.
26 Edith-Stein Gesellschaft Deutschland
Postfach 16 49
67326 Speyer
GERMANY

INDEX

Bold faced numerals refer to main entries

Courant,
Adelheid, 51, 52, 54, 71, 73, 158, 171
Clara, 93, 96, 151
David, 39, 104, 105, 132
Emil, 55
Friederike, 96
Jakob, 38
Nellie, née Neumann, 112, 117, 118
Richard, 51, 112, 115, 117, 118, 194
Salomon, 51, 52, 54, 55, 71, 73
Domincan Sisters of St. Magdelena in Speyer, 207
Dreyfus Affair, 45
Drügemöller, Hedwig (Teresia Margareta vom Herzen Jesu) OCD, 176
Edict of Emancipation, April 16, 1871, p. 43
Edict of Emanciaption, Prussia, March 11, 1812, 38-40
Edith Stein Center at Spalding University, 208
Edith Stein Guild, New York, 208
Edith Stein Jahrbuch (Yearbook), 210
Edith Stein Society of Germany, Speyer, 210
Edith Stein Society of Lubliniec, 53, 209
Edith Stein Society of Wroclaw, 90, 94, 98, 209
Fränkel, Zacharias, 42
Friedrich-Wilhelm-Universität, Breslau, 31, 32
Frings, Josef, Cardinal, 21, 176
Funeral customs, Jewish, 190
Gelber , Lucie, 174, 175
Gleiwitz, 49, 50, 55, 73, 148
Good Friday prayer, 15
Gordon
Else, née Stein, 57-60, 64-67, 80-81, 192
Marriage, 65-66, 80-81
Ilse, 64, 67, 80, 120
Max, 64, 65, 66, 67, 80, 81, 112, 116
Werner, 64, 81, 82, 205
Hamburg, 64-66, 77, 80, 81, 112, 120, 192
Heil im Unheil (Well-Being in the Midst of Disaster), 179
Herbstrith, Waltraud, OCD (Maria Teresia), 67, 207
Herrmann, Adele OP, 207
Herzl, Theodor, 44
Hochschule für die Wissenschaft des Judentums, 39
Horowitz,
Franz, 93, 132, 183, 191
Hans, 93, 132
Selma, née Courant, 93
Humani Generis Unitas, 200
Husserl, Edmund, 19, 101, 111-115, 118, 172, 173, 186
Ingarden, Roman, 185
Jägerstrasse 5, (now ul. Mysliwska) p. 58
Jahn, Friedrich Ludwig (Turnvater), 37, 44
Jahrhunderthalle (now Hala Ludowa), 34

Svensson, Jan, 125
Synagogue *Zum weissen, Storch*, 40, 41
Teresia Margareta vom Herzen Jesu, Sr. OCD (Hedwig Drügemöller), 176
Teresia Renata Sr. OCD (Teresia Renata Posselt), 83, 95
Theresienstadt (also Terezin), 97, 124, 151-153, 156, 167
Treitschke, Heinrich von, 44
Triumphalism, Christian, 16
Tworoger,
    Elfriede, née Stein, 62, 79, 151, **153-156,** 160, 161, 167
        Marriage, 153-154
    Erika, (later Hannah Cohen), 90, 97, 121, 126, 153-154, 160
Viadrina, 32, 43
Vier Türme [Four Towers], 97
Villa Nova, 55
Vogelstein, Herrmann, Rabbi 40
We Remember: A Reflection on the Shoah, 202
Women students at Breslau University, 102-103, 105, 113, 192
Women, Jewish, 191
Women's Student Union, 105
World Eucharistic Congress, 99
Zentralrat der Juden in Deutschland (Central Council of Jews in Germany), 46
Zionist Congress, first, 45
Zionist Union in Germany, 45

Other Edith Stein Books

Edith Stein: Selected Writings
*With Comments, Reminiscences
and Translations of her Prayers
and Poems by her niece
Susanne Batzdorff*
ISBN 0-87243-189-4

An Edith Stein Daybook
*To Live at the Hand of the Lord
Translated by
Susanne Batzdorff*
ISBN 0-87243-206-8